D1487879

You can *Write a* Movie

Pamela Wallace

WRITER'S DIGEST BOOKS
CINCINNATI, OHIO
www.writersdigest.com

Visit our Web site at www.writersdigest.com for information on more resources for writers.

To receive a free weekly E-mail newsletter delivering tips and updates about writing and about Writer's Digest products, send an E-mail with "Subscribe Newsletter" in the body of the message to newsletter-request@writersdigest.com or register directly at our Web site at www.writersdigest.com.

04   03   02   01   00   5   4   3   2   1

Library of Congress Cataloging-in-Publication Data

Wallace, Pamela.
  You can write a movie / by Pamela Wallace.
    p.   cm.
  Includes index.
  ISBN 0-89879-974-0
    1. Motion picture authorship. I. Title.

PN1996.W23   2000
808.2'3—dc21
                                  00-036487
                                   CIP

Editors: Jack Heffron and Meg Leder
Cover photography: Beau Regard/Masterfile
Production coordinator: Mark Griffin

To my son, Christopher,
the most talented writer I've ever known.

ACKNOWLEDGMENTS

Film is a collaborative medium. I've had the good fortune to work with many intelligent, insightful and enormously creative people in the film business, including fellow writers, directors, producers, actors and executives. They've helped me grow enormously as a writer and a human being— and they've improved my work significantly. I must single out two people, without whose professional support and friendship, I wouldn't be where I am today as a writer: Kathie Fong Yoneda and Madeline DiMaggio. A heartfelt thank-you.

Pam Wallace began writing screenplays in the mid-1980s, and in 1985 she won an Academy Award for co-writing the movie *Witness*. She has written or co-written several other films, including the award-winning HBO film *If These Walls Could Talk*, the CBS movie of the week *Borrowed Hearts* (which was the highest-rated television program of the week it aired), and the ABC movies of the week *Lovers of Deceit* and *Alibi*.

In addition, Wallace has published more than twenty-five novels, several of which have been optioned or produced as movies of the week, miniseries or made-for-cable movies. Her novels have been translated into a dozen languages, and one of them, *Fortune's Child*, won the Reviewers' Choice Award for Best Contemporary Novel.

She lives in Fresno, California.

TABLE OF CONTENTS

PART ONE

Before You Write Your Screenplay

PART TWO

Writing Your Screenplay

In my twenty-plus years of evaluating more than seventeen thousand screenplays, books, treatments, plays, manuscripts and pitches, for several of the top studios in Hollywood, I've often wished for a magical handbook that could give both novice and struggling screenwriters a concise, no-nonsense primer on the basic "craft" of writing scripts for motion pictures and television, coupled with the realities of breaking into the entertainment business. With Pamela Wallace's *You Can Write a Movie*, it looks like my wish has been granted! And what makes things even better is that this magical guide has been written by someone who's experienced both the highs and lows of scripting, and has survived and thrived through it all.

Pam's look into the somewhat hazy, undefined world of film and television writing is practical, yet insightful, and always truthful. She's the first one to tell you that winning an Oscar doesn't guarantee a lifetime of lucrative writing assignments, but she's also quick to let you know that with each project written, the journey becomes less frightening. It is filled with lessons that can help you shape and improve your work and enhance your growth as a writer and storyteller of the human experience.

Now, whenever a writer, executive, producer or client asks if there's a "magic" book on screenwriting, I can confidently direct them to *You Can Write a Movie*, and tell them that while they will ultimately have to supply their own brand of "magic," this book can be their touchstone.

Kathie Fong Yoneda
Story Analyst, Paramount Studio

The first theatrical screenplay I ever wrote, *Witness* (co-written with Earl W. Wallace and William Kelley), was rejected by everyone—studios, production companies, actors—for three years. During that time, I decided that everyone else must be right and I must be wrong. It wasn't as good as I thought it was. Finally, unexpectedly, it sold when Harrison Ford agreed to star in it. It was immediately produced, won an Academy Award the following year, and was recently named one of the top fifty movies of all time.

I learned three things from that experience. One, I needed to believe in myself a heck of a lot more. Two, when you write from the heart, you touch other people's hearts. And three, I was a novice screenwriter who happened to capture "lightning in a bottle" before I had truly learned the craft. As a friend said at that time, "It's like getting a college degree without attending classes. Now you have to go back and learn what you don't know." I spent the next ten years doing just that: reading about screenwriting; working with experienced writers, directors, actors and producers; learning from them; and writing script after script. Some of them sold, but weren't produced. Some sold, were produced, but weren't very successful. And a couple were produced and were quite successful.

Along the way, I painstakingly learned the craft of screenwriting. I am still learning it every day, with every page I write, because writing is a journey, not a destination. But I know a great deal more now than I did when I stepped up onto that stage before millions of people and said nervously, "I'd like to thank the members of the Academy. . . ." This book is my way of sharing what I have learned. It's written as clearly as possible, so that a novice screenwriter can understand it, but it also deals with sophisticated insights that even experienced screenwriters will find useful. In short, it covers everything you need to know to write and market a screenplay.

Beyond the craft lessons about structure and characterization, theme and dialogue, this book includes the insights I've gained about the film business, especially why scripts do or do not sell. Most importantly, it has something most books on screenwriting don't have because they're not written by writers—firsthand knowledge about the act of creation itself. There are many excellent books on the craft of screenwriting. Almost all of these books are written by people who are terrific teachers, with a great deal of useful information to impart. But they can't tell you what it's like to actually struggle through the writing process, from the standpoint of a working writer. This book will do just that.

I hope the information you gain here will erase any doubts you may have about your ability to write a screenplay. I firmly believe that everyone who has the desire to write has at least one compelling story in them, probably more. It's simply a question of learning the craft and doing the hard work of actually writing.

Finally, I hope this book will inspire you to write a story that just may capture "lightning in a bottle" for you, too.

PART ONE

Before You Write Your Screenplay

1 Getting Ideas

Jeffrey Katzenberg is one of the three owners of DreamWorks studio (the other two being the incomparable director-producer Steven Spielberg and music mogul David Geffen). For many years he was a top executive at Disney Studios. While there, he wrote a famous memo that was intended for internal use, but nevertheless became widely disseminated throughout the industry. It was the ultimate "insider" look at what studio executives look for (or should look for) in a screenplay. In essence he said this: *the idea is king.*

Katzenberg wrote that stars, directors, writers, hardware and special effects can influence the success of a film. But these elements only work if they serve a good idea. If a movie is based on an entertaining, emotionally compelling, original idea, chances are it will succeed, even if it isn't executed brilliantly. But a movie based on a flawed idea will almost always fail, despite the presence of "A" talent and an aggressive marketing campaign.

The memo discusses the common phrase "high concept." This was coined to describe a fresh idea whose originality could be conveyed briefly as in, a small band of brave men must risk their lives in a suicide mission to save the earth from being obliterated by an approaching asteroid (*Armageddon*). If you can't explain the essence of a story in one or two lines, it isn't high concept. High concept links moviemaking and movie marketing. The story is easy to understand and easy to sell to an audience. Katzenberg believed that the real meaning of "high concept" is that an ingenious idea is more critical than expensive production values. (Recently, the term "high concept" has been supplanted by "unique concept," to indicate that there's something very fresh and different—but not *too* different—about the story.)

According to Katzenberg, while the idea is king and high concept is powerful, it's crucial to translate them into compelling stories. What makes a story compelling? A central character who goes through a transforming experience with which the audience can relate. In *Raiders of the Lost Ark*, Indiana Jones's cockiness is humbled by the realization that there are forces even he shouldn't challenge. *Tootsie* is about a man who becomes a better man by pretending to be a woman. A successful story will stir emotions in its viewers, making them laugh or cry (or both in really good movies), shriek in horror or simply be moved by what they're seeing on the screen.

What Katzenberg was basically talking about is the importance of the universal appeal of an idea. Most successful films express an underlying idea that has universal appeal to most audiences. This idea causes audiences to identify with the characters and situations, by either showing them an experience they've had or by showing them an experience they'd *like* to have.

Usually such an idea can be expressed very simply: underdog triumphs (*The Karate Kid*) . . . revenge (*Dirty Harry*) . . . triumph of the human spirit (*The Color Purple*) . . . coming-of-age (*Stand by Me*). Such simple ideas make connections with audience members. The great English novelist E.M. Forster said, "Only connect." That is the mandate of every successful film. To accomplish that, you need an idea that people will feel an emotional connection to.

When studio executives or producers talk about what kinds of stories they're looking for, they invariably focus on the basic idea of the movie. Is the story "castable?" In other words, are the leading roles appropriate for "bankable" stars? Or is the idea strong enough that you don't need stars (as in *Independence Day*)? Has this idea proved commercial in the past? Or, even better, is it a fresh take on a proven commodity?

And most of all, is it an idea that appeals to the broadest possible demographic? With the cost of making and marketing movies soaring astronomically (typically exceeding $100 or $200 million for big summer releases), a movie can't just appeal to a small core audience. It has to expand. As one marketing executive at a major studio says, "A mainstream release needs to reach at least two major segments of the moviegoing public. You can't afford to narrowcast."

The typical studio strategy is to target a primary audience first, then go after a secondary and possibly tertiary group. *George of the Jungle* is a quintessential example. Ostensibly, it was made for little kids. After all, it was based on a cartoon. But the sexy Brendan Fraser wearing nothing but a loincloth combined with a witty script decidedly adult in some of its humor,

5

turned the broad comedy into a must-see event for teens and an enjoyable entertainment for adults (especially women).

The power of the basic idea of a film is clearly illustrated in the list of movies that have the best profit vs. cost ratio. Every year, at the top of this list are "small" films without big stars or huge budgets that nevertheless make a bigger profit than much more high-profile movies. In 1997 a little British movie that cost a mere $3.5 million to produce was the top revenue ratio champ—*The Full Monty*. In fact, that year's top five films in terms of profit were each made for under $6 million. If they didn't have "bankable" stars or expensive special effects, why were they successful? Because the basic concept of the movie was so appealing to a vast audience. This fact alone demonstrates that Katzenberg is right—the idea *is* king.

So now you know what kind of idea you need to come up with. But where do the best ideas come from? How do you recognize those that have the potential to be a great movie, and those that don't? Does inspiration play a role in conceiving a great film? If so, where do you find that elusive muse?

These questions haunt every writer, both the novice and the old pro. I am continually asked, "Where do you get your ideas from?" I'm tempted to answer, "From Ideas 'R' Us, of course." Actually, I'm one of those fortunate writers who has no shortage of ideas—only a shortage of time in which to write them. Where do my ideas come from? A variety of sources—reading a newspaper or magazine article, looking at my own life or the lives of my friends or people in the news, fantasizing about something I wish I could experience but know that in reality I never will.

Specifically, *Witness* came about when I read a newspaper article about the Amish and was amazed that people lived such simple lives in a complex world. The article was about an Amish baby who was accidentally killed when non-Amish teenage boys threw rocks at the carriage the baby was in. Having a baby of my own at the time, my heart went out to the parents. The idea for my CBS movie, *Borrowed Hearts,* came when I started thinking about what I had most wanted as a child and didn't have—a father. I wrote three romance novels that were made into movies for the Showtime channel as a result of letting my most wildly romantic imaginings run amok.

What every movie I've done has in common is the fact that a subject or thought touched my heart. I related to it personally and wanted to explore the feelings it evoked deep within me. I've tried to write stories that are coldly calculated. *Action movies are selling—fine, I'll just whip out one of those blockbusters.* Unfortunately, that doesn't work for me. I don't believe it works for most writers. That isn't to say that every writer feels a deep passion for every movie he writes. But I strongly believe that in most cases, for an audience to love a movie, the writer has to first love what he's writing.

The greatest success I've known as a screenwriter has been with stories that were heartfelt. The greatest failure has come when I tried to write what I thought the market would buy, even though it didn't appeal to me.

Write from the heart.

Write with passion.

The money—or, at least, a tremendous sense of pride and fulfillment—will follow.

Where do you find inspiration for such ideas? In your own heart and mind. Did you read about an event, or witness one, that touched you deeply? Did someone you know have an experience or express an intimate feeling that touched you deeply? Is there an issue that is profoundly disturbing to you? Explore these feelings. There is an idea for a movie there—a movie you will care deeply about, and therefore other people may care deeply about, as well.

But, you say, there are a great many things that touch you deeply. How do you judge which idea has enough potential to make it worthy of investing time and effort to turn it into a movie? If an idea genuinely excites you, there is a good chance it will excite an audience—if it's developed properly. The key is to be clear about what it is exactly that excites you about that idea, and don't lose track of that while writing the script.

In my experience the best indication that I'm on to a viable idea for a movie lies in the sudden jolt of excitement I feel when I first conceive it. It's literally heartfelt—I feel deep emotion welling up within me when I think of the emotional power of the idea. It's the kind of thing that makes you grab the nearest pen and hurriedly jot down the bare bones of the concept before you forget it. Or tune out everything and everyone else while you focus on the newspaper article or TV news item that has struck you with such force.

Recognizing an idea with real film potential is part inspiration and part physical sensation, and it points to the essence of your creative excitement about a potential story. It's critical to hold onto this, because therein lies the "true north" of your story. Lose sight of it, and your story won't be as powerful as it could have been. If you hold fast in your memory the feeling you had when the idea first came to you, then you can communicate that feeling to an audience.

The best ideas often are the most intimate and personal, and therefore the hardest to access or hold on to. Subconsciously, we resist fully feeling that particular sensation because it's painful or frightening. But a deeply held personal truth is the basis for the greatest films. At the very least, it's the basis for a movie that will profoundly touch an audience.

When *Borrowed Hearts* sold to a production company (after being rejected for three years), the executive at the company asked me how I came up with the idea. I was terribly embarrassed to admit the genesis of this particular idea. I said, "You're going to think I'm crazy, but . . . and I proceeded to reluctantly explain how this story of a man who "rents" a family for business purposes, then falls in love with the single mother and her young daughter, came about. My therapist wanted me to "get in touch with my inner child." I felt foolish trying to have a dialogue with an invisible version of my much younger self. I couldn't do it. However, I could do what writers do all the time—write about those feelings that I was so uncomfortable with expressing verbally. I asked myself what I would have given to myself as a child, if I could have given anything. The answer was simple— the father I didn't have.

From there, it was relatively simple to come up with a plot. I chose the romantic comedy/drama genre because it's my favorite type of movie. I devised a conflict-filled relationship between the hero and heroine that was nicely romantic. But the focus of the story was definitely the little girl and her evolving relationship with the man who initially didn't want to have a family. By the time he rescues her physically at the end, she has taught him how to love and rescued his soul.

Borrowed Hearts was the number-one-rated TV program of the week it aired, and the fourth-highest-rated TV movie of the season. All of that from a simple but profound longing for the father I never had.

When you fight your way through the difficulties of writing a screenplay, always go back to the power of the initial idea. Why did it touch you? What do you want to express in the story? Never lose sight of that.

Your own personal, emotional approach to an idea makes it uniquely yours. No other writer would explore that particular story exactly as you would. Your internal associations with an idea make it powerful. A plot is nothing without the passion you bring to it, and that passion springs from how you felt when you first conceived the idea.

2 Genres

One of the first questions a studio executive or producer will ask about a screenplay is, "Which genre does it fall into?" They ask this question for two reasons. First, they need to know what their expectations should be before reading the script. (If they find themselves laughing, but it's supposed to be a drama, they know something is *very* wrong.) Second, they can make a preliminary judgment about the marketability of the script. They know that a limited number of genres—action/adventure, broad comedy and sci-fi/fantasy—tend to have the greatest commercial potential.

Every movie falls into a category or genre. Here's a complete list, compliments of Paramount story analyst Kathie Fong Yoneda:

Action	Ecology
Adventure	Espionage/Intrigue
Alcohol/Drug Abyse ✓	Fantasy ✓
Animal	Family
Biography/Autobiography	Family Relations
Business	Family Saga
Caper	Farce
Character Study	Gambling
College/High School/Teen ✓	Gangster/Organized Crime
Comedy	Historical
Coming-of-Age ✓	Holocaust
Computer/High Tech	Horror
Costume Drama	Juvenile
Courtroom	Labor
Crime	Medical
Detective	Melodrama
Disaster	Midlife Crisis
Docudrama	Military
Drama	Multicultural

Musical	Sea
Mystery	Sexual Themes
Nazi/Neo-Nazi	Sexploitation
Newspaper	Show Business
Nostalgia	Soap Opera
Occult War	Spoof
Police	Sports
Political	Subculture
Prison	Suspense-Thriller
Religion	Terrorist
Revenge	Tragedy
Romance	Utopia
Romantic Comedy	War
Satire	Western
Sci-Fi	Women
Sci-Fantasy	

It is literally impossible to come up with a story that doesn't fit into one or more of these categories. An analysis of the ten top-grossing films of 1999 shows how every movie falls into an easily identifiable genre.

Star Wars: Episode I—The Phantom Menace—sci-fi/fantasy/action
The Sixth Sense—spiritual/drama/suspense
Austin Powers: The Spy Who Shagged Me—comedy/action
Toy Story 2—comedy/fantasy
The Matrix—sci-fi/action/thriller
Tarzan—romantic/adventure/musical/historical
Big Daddy—romantic/comedy/family
The Mummy—action/horror/historical
Runaway Bride—romantic/comedy
The Blair Witch Project—horror/suspense/drama

As you can see, most successful movies combine genres; however, be careful about which genres you combine. We've all had the experience of watching a movie that "doesn't know what it wants to be." Perhaps it starts out as a light comedy, then turns grimly dramatic. Only the most brilliant filmmaker can combine something as serious as the holocaust with comedy (*Life Is Beautiful*).

If you find yourself blocked, unable to think of a story that you feel passionate about, look over this list. Find a genre that you like, where you feel your strengths as a writer would best be displayed. A few great writers are eclectic and can work in many different genres, but most writers have a particular area of interest that ignites their passion. Ask yourself what your favorite genre is. Focus on that area, at least at the start of your career. Once you've written enough scripts to master a genre, and, hopefully, have sold one or more of them, then you might consider testing your abilities in other genres.

After determining the genre you want to work within, the next step is to understand the rules of that particular genre. How well you follow those rules will determine the success or failure of your screenplay. Each genre has certain conventions and elicits certain expectations from the audience. For instance, the audience always expects a romantic comedy to have a happy ending. The formula is boy-meets-girl, boy-loses-girl, boy-gets-girl; fade out on a kiss. A western will always be set in the American West of the 1800s (even if it's a "spaghetti western," actually shot in Italy), and the good guys and the bad guys will end up in a shoot-out. A crime story will always focus on criminals who may or may not get away with the crime.

After roughly one hundred years of moviegoing, the audience knows these conventions and expects to see them fulfilled. These conventions determine what can and cannot happen within a story.

Some genres are more flexible than others. A writer has wide latitude when it comes to drama, for instance. But other genres have narrow and rigid conventions. In a thriller, there must be a personal element. *Ransom* would have been a far less compelling story if the kidnapped child wasn't the son of the protagonist.

Even comedy, which can encompass a broad variety of stories, has one overriding convention—the main characters can't be seriously hurt. Though, like the Wile E. Coyote cartoon character, they can be battered repeatedly. The comedy writer may put his character through endless torments, but the audience must not feel that there's serious pain involved. Even in black comedy, the events might be quite edgy, but still not unbearably dark.

How do you learn the conventions of a genre? Select several movies, preferably successful ones, that are like the story you want to tell. Rent the films on video and buy the screenplays. Keep a notebook and pen handy, and analyze the movies as you watch them—setting, characters, plot. List each major scene in order so you can see the progression of the plot. Look for the similarities in all these movies. What events always happen in them? This tells you what the audience's expectations are for that particular genre.

If a movie is accurately promoted (as opposed to trying to trick the audience into thinking it's one thing when it's really another), the audience will come to it with a sense of what they're about to see. This is referred to by marketing experts as "positioning the movie." The audience knows what to expect, and if the movie delivers, it's a success.

Once, I invited a friend to watch *The Elephant Man* with me. She knew nothing about it, but somehow was under the impression it was a comedy. When she found herself watching a serious drama with a sad ending, she was completely caught off-guard. Even though it was a brilliant and deeply touching film that both critics and audiences loved, my friend didn't like it. She had been expecting one thing and got another. She wasn't emotionally prepared (or "positioned?") for the movie.

If you're thinking that it sounds like there's a formula for every genre, you're right. The challenge to the writer is to take that formula and somehow make it fresh and surprising and entertaining. You must honor the conventions, meet the audience's expectations—but avoid cliche.

An executive once said that the closest thing to a surefire success is a story that is a fresh take on an established genre. *Sleepless in Seattle* is a perfect example. It fulfilled the conventions of the romantic/comedy genre, but with a twist—the hero and heroine didn't meet until the last scene.

As you can see, combining genres can add layers of depth and meaning to a story, and make the characters more complex. A cross-cultural love story turned what was otherwise just another police thriller into an exceptional film (*Witness*). Music made a slight horror film a cult classic (*The Rocky Horror Picture Show*).

Genres evolve over time. As society changes, so do movies. The western was dated and predictable until Mel Brooks hilariously reinvented it in *Blazing Saddles*, poking fun at the conventions the audience knew so well. Clint Eastwood reinvented it again in *Unforgiven* by making the "hero" a deeply flawed, all-too-human man. And Kevin Costner elevated the genre beyond its often racist attitudes by depicting Indians sympathetically in *Dances With Wolves*.

The Love Story

One of the most popular genres of all time, the love story, is very challenging to update. At a time when there are very few "rules" keeping people apart, how do you separate your hero and heroine for most of the movie? The basic conflict in a love story is, what's stopping them from getting together? Finding a fresh new barrier to love is difficult. In *Witness*, it was the heroine's culture that was the barrier—she was Amish, virtually from a different world than the hero. In *Ghost*, it was the ultimate barrier—death.

In *When Harry Met Sally*, the barrier was an expression of contemporary thought—men and women can't combine sex and friendship. Romantic comedies, perhaps more than many other genres, are reflections of their times. The barrier keeping the hero and heroine apart must seem realistic and compelling to an audience watching it at the time the movie is made.

Perhaps the most important reason to pick a genre you love, study it, then write in it, is that this will inspire you to remain excited about the story throughout the long haul of writing it and then enduring the almost inevitable rejection that follows. Very few screenplays sell to the first buyer who reads them. The vast majority, even those that go on to become critical and commercial successes, meet with repeated rejection. Writing a good movie is difficult and time-consuming. Marketing it is fraught with disappointment and frustration. What keeps you going throughout this physically and emotionally trying process, is loving the story you're writing. The admonition, "Focus on the process and don't have an attachment to the outcome," is far easier to do if your passion is fully engaged and you're writing the story you want to write, as opposed to one you think you *should* write.

Loglines and Premises

The first step in actually writing a film is to concisely define the content of your story. Whether you call it theme, premise, substance or text, it all means one thing—the ethical or moral point of the movie. One of the most scathing comments an audience member can make as he leaves a theater is, "What on earth was that all about"?

To avoid such confusion, there's a simple but critical solution. Encapsulate your idea in a one- or two-line description. This is commonly referred to as the "logline," as in the *TV Guide* log, wherein one or two sentences explain the essence of the plots of TV shows. Lajos Egri, the author of the brilliant book *The Art of Dramatic Writing*, strongly urges writers to boil down your story's meaning into a single sentence. That may sound impossible, but it really isn't. A good story is usually a human experience that reflects a principle or theme that can be stated succinctly.

Here are a couple of examples of how a single sentence can express the underlying principle of a movie.

- *The Hospital* (Academy Award-winning screenplay by Paddy Chayefsky): "A doctor's duty to his patients transcends his personal concerns and comforts."
- *Othello*: "Jealousy consumes a man, driving him to destroy the one he loves."

If you can't express the essence of your story in one or, at most, two or three lines, then it lacks focus. The point of a logline isn't to explain all the details of a movie. It's to convey a sense of what kind of story it is, who it's about and what's at stake.

When the industry trade paper *Daily Variety* writes an article about a script, book or "pitch" that's sold, there is usually a logline describing the story. A recent one said: "A backwoods legend and a female park ranger team up to defeat powerful industrial polluters in the magnificent mountains of northern Michigan." In that one line we learn who the movie is about (a backwoods legend and a female park ranger), what the conflict is about (industrial pollution), who the villain is (a big business) and the setting (the magnificent mountains of northern Michigan).

From that logline we know what kind of movie it is—an action/adventure, probably with romantic overtones—and that it's highly castable. What actor wouldn't want to play a "backwoods legend"? And what actress wouldn't be interested in playing a fairly unusual role for a female, a park ranger?

Another recent *Daily Variety* article described a "pitch" that sold this way: " 'Jackson' is a sentimental drama about a young man who accidentally causes another man's death. The man goes through a mysterious transformation that causes him to bring closure to many of the unresolved issues in the life of the dead man. He is then forced to reevaluate his own life choices."

It's easy to see why this as-yet-unwritten story sold for well over a million dollars. The moral elements of the story—taking responsibility for our actions, healing, finding closure—are very compelling. The stakes are ones an audience will care about—the protagonist's spiritual salvation and healing the people hurt by the man's death. It's highly castable. Any number of hot young actors would love to portray a character who goes through this kind of growth and change, especially since he is ultimately heroic.

Also, it's important to note that the traditional three-act structure is clearly apparent in this logline. In Act One, the setup, the protagonist accidentally kills a man. In Act Two, the complications, he tries to make amends, undergoes a spiritual transformation and helps the people involved with the victim. And in Act Three, the resolution, he makes changes in his own life.

Laura Ziskin, the highly successful executive producer of *Pretty Woman*, among other movies, and the head of the Fox 2000 division of Twentieth Century Fox studio, had this to say about casting: "I think one criteria in today's world that is always in the front of my mind from the inception of an idea, is casting. Because sometimes there's a great story about, you know, a sixty-year-old man and a fifty-year-old woman, and it may be a great *story*, but I may think to myself, 'Can we cast it?' And then we're always thinking about the marketplace. 'Who is this movie for? Who is it going to appeal to?' "

Your logline should give a clear sense of the castability of the characters and the marketability of the plot. If not, your screenplay is probably going to be difficult to sell.

William Mechanic, chair and CEO of Fox Filmed Entertainment, elaborated on Ms. Ziskin's comment: "When you put something in development,

15

the only question you're asking is, 'Is it a movie?' And then, 'Who is it a movie for?' and then you start to make your decisions from there. But your first assertion is always that very basic question, 'Is this a movie? Is this a movie I want to see? Is this a movie *somebody* wants to see? Is it a movie *how many* people will want to see?' And if it's very expensive, and it's a good script you ask, 'OK, is it a movie that will attract one of those ten [marketable] people? Or is the idea strong enough that, like *Independence Day*, you don't need stars?' If it's not one of those two things, it's no longer a movie. It's just an expensive script."

Both Ms. Ziskin and Mr. Mechanic were discussing major studio motion pictures. Jack Lechner, executive vice president, production and development, Miramax Films (a major independent production company), was referring to the independent, or lower-budget film market when he said, "If it's a niche movie, does it have a unique selling proposition, as they say in another industry? Is it something that has something remarkable?"

There are lessons to be learned about why some premises work—i.e., the screenplay sells, is produced and is commercially and/or critically successful—and some don't.

Fatal flaws in a premise:

- It's silly and unbelievable—except in a broad comedy, in which case the sillier the better. *There's Something About Mary* is a case in point.
- It's a limited idea that doesn't allow for enough plot development or surprises (too linear and predictable).
- It's an idea that is offensive in some way—demeaning, racist, sexist or too crude even for a hip audience open to edgy fare. (*Indiana Jones and the Temple of Doom* was the least successful movie in the *Indiana Jones* trilogy because it was widely felt to be offensive in some scenes, especially to the broad audience it was intended for.)
- It's a concept audiences can't identify with.

Strong elements in a premise:

- It should explore a topic that could change your life; for instance, dealing with an issue that affects you deeply and with which you're trying to come to terms. Writing truly is the best therapy. If you write about something meaningful to you, then the process hasn't been a waste of time, even if the script never sells.
- Your protagonist should be your best (strongest, most interesting) character. Do you love this character, and also, at times, hate him?

- The central conflict should be absolutely clear and compelling. Who's fighting who about what? And why should an audience care?
- There should be a single primary cause-and-effect line in the story. If there is a split, where the story goes offtrack, the story will lose focus.
- There should be a central moral choice to be made by the protagonist. He must choose between two compelling and desirable possibilities. If one is negative and one is positive, the choice is too easy. For example, in *Air Force One*, the president, played by Harrison Ford, must choose between his family's safety and the welfare of the country. Because he's our hero, he's able to find a way to save his family and do the right thing for the country, at great risk to himself, of course.
- The story line must be unique enough, or at least present a fresh take on an established idea, to be interesting.

A logline gives you an opportunity to assess the strengths and weaknesses of your premise, not only in terms of its commerciality, but in terms of its creative value. If what's at stake in the premise isn't strong enough to capture the hearts and minds of an audience, you know you need to dig deeper into your story.

I've asked several people in the film industry—story analysts, producers, network and studio executives—what they feel is the single most common reason why a screenplay is rejected. They all agreed that it was simple: what was at stake in the story simply wasn't compelling enough. It's the "who cares" issue. If the logline I mentioned earlier about the "backwoods legend" and female park ranger had been about a minor infraction instead of industrial pollution of a magnificent natural setting, the screenplay wouldn't have sold.

A great way to determine a stake for a story is to ask yourself what you care deeply about. If you care about children, then writing a family drama about an abused child will be emotionally compelling. If you care about the environment, an ecologically oriented adventure story about the threat to a fragile ecosystem could be dramatic. You must be interested in the subject matter and care deeply about the point of the story for an audience to care.

4 Formatting a Screenplay

Once, an acquaintance asked me to read a screenplay he had written. I took one look at the first page and pointed out that the script wasn't in proper format. He replied with naive nonchalance, "I know. I didn't want to be bound by those rules. I wanted to do it my way." As soon as I heard that, I politely but firmly told him I couldn't read his script. If he wasn't willing to follow the rules, it was a waste of my time to read it because no one else would, either.

Before I explain the "rules" of proper screenplay format, I want to say a word about the overall appearance of your script. A professional-looking script begins with a title page, listing only the title, your name, and at the bottom your address and phone number, or your agent's name and number. Do not put a copyright notice, Writers Guild of America registration number, a date or any indication of which draft of the script you're submitting. If the script is based on a book, indicate this by writing under your name, "Based on (title of book) by (author)." If you're writing with a collaborator, insert an ampersand (&) between both names, not "and."

Give the script a plain front and back cover (do not use fancy artwork). Punch three holes in standard fashion on the left-hand side of the page at the top, middle and bottom. Bind it with two, not three, brass, round-head fasteners, usually two inches long. (Two is standard operating procedure. If you use three, you'll betray your lack of professional status.)

There are any number of good software programs that will automatically format your screenplay. I highly recommend using one, because it will make your writing much faster and simpler. I use Final Draft, one of the most commonly used programs, but there are many other good ones.

However, if you don't choose to use a screenwriting program, there is a simple, easy-to-learn format for writing screenplays. Any script that arrives at the office of an agent, producer, or studio or network executive, has to be properly formatted, or it will betray the amateur status of the writer and won't be considered. Some estimates suggest that as many as 100,000 screenplays per year are submitted to agencies, studios, networks and production companies. There aren't nearly enough employees to read all those scripts, so before bothering to read them, they discard as many as possible for the most readily apparent reason: They don't *look* professional.

As I've said earlier, a great way to learn how to write a screenplay is to read them. But keep in mind that when you read a script purchased from a company that sells them, you're often getting a "shooting" script. It may very well have numbered scenes, camera angles, directive parentheticals and technical information that help in budgeting and shooting a film. That's not something you should do with your script. Yours should be easy to read, with almost no camera angles (directors don't like to be told how to direct) except where absolutely necessary, no technical information unless it's essential for the reader to understand the story, and very few parentheticals (actors don't like to be told how to act).

Here are the rules for proper screenplay formatting.

Margins for Script Format

	Left Margin	Right Margin
Scene Description	2″	1½″
Dialogue	3″	2″
Parenthetical	3½″	2½″
Character Name	4″	

Page Number: ½″ down; ½″ from right margin.

Typing must never go beyond the right margin.

If you are using a font that equals ten characters per inch, your scene description must be within the fifty spaces allowed between margins 20 (2″ left) and 70 (1½″ right).

Dialogue must be within the thirty-five spaces (3″ left; 2″ right).

Parentheticals (description in parenthesis under the character's name) must be within twenty-five spaces (3½″ left; 2½″ right).

Page number will be on line four.

Start typing on line six.

Between scenes, leave three blank spaces from the last line of typing; type on the fourth.

Directions

In the directions, always capitalize any camera angles or sound effects.

Following are the most commonly used directions.

P.O.V. (Point of View): If you want to indicate that a shot is to be from the same perspective as the character who is seeing it—for instance, a character named Pamela—write PAMELA'S P.O.V. In essence, the camera is behind that character and what we see onscreen is what that character sees.

V.O. (Voice-Over): This is used when we can hear the character's voice but can't see him. Often this is used in telephone conversations between characters and when a character is talking over a scene that he isn't in, most commonly when one scene "dissolves into" another. A V.O. is also used if you see a car moving down the street and hear the voices of the occupants but don't see them.

O.S. (Offscreen): This is used when we hear a sound but don't see what's causing it; e.g., when a character is sitting in his living room and he hears his front door slam shut as someone leaves the house. It can be written like this: O.S. MUSIC FROM ORCHESTRA, or O.S. INDISTINCT PARTY SOUNDS.

B.G. (Background): This is usually part of the description of a scene. For example, "As a couple walks down the beach, in the B.G. we see a dog playing in the surf."

CUT TO: In the past this was used to indicate that you were cutting quickly from one scene to another. Nowadays, it isn't used much.

DISSOLVE TO (or DISSOLVE THROUGH TO): This is used at the end of a scene to suggest a slow change from one scene to another, often a change in time or place. For instance, you might have a scene about a child focusing on a brand new toy. Then you DISSOLVE TO the next scene, showing the toy as old and battered, indicating a passage of time and the growth of the child.

INSERT: This can be used to show a close-up of a significant object inserted into a scene. For instance, you would INSERT a knife tucked into a belt, to suggest a threat, as a criminal approaches a victim he's about to attack.

The Business

The description of a scene, and the action indicated, are commonly referred to as "the business" of a screenplay. This includes the description of the setting and all the choreography of the actions of the characters (for example, "John walks to the door, hesitates, then flings it open"). There are rules about this, just as there are rules about formatting. You need to keep "the business" short and to the point, but at the same time vivid and exciting. If it's boring, the reader of your script will lose interest. Don't use elaborate descriptions. Only write what the camera will actually show. Flowery descriptions belong in novels, not screenplays.

Write directions in single-spaced prose paragraphs, flush with the left-hand margin. Like the entire script, write it in pica type, ten spaces to the inch. Do not use smaller type. Write in present tense, as if we're seeing it onscreen at that moment. Use direction to introduce and describe characters. Write most of a character's physical description when he is first introduced. Make that description vivid but brief.

Since "the business" must translate into a movie, make it interesting to read by using active verbs and strong action words. One of the biggest lessons I learned when I made the transition from being a novelist to being a screenwriter was that in describing a scene, I couldn't tell what a character was thinking or feeling, only what he was doing.

Ideally, a direction paragraph should be short, no more than a few lines. (Readers look for lots of "white space" in a script, which means not a lot of dense writing. It should be roughly 50–50 between ink and white space.) Always double-space to the new direction paragraph.

Even though most screenplays follow the traditional three-act structure, don't indicate these acts in the script. An exception to this rule is TV movies, which are usually seven acts long (except for certain cable channels that break down their movies into eight acts). With TV movies, indicate act breaks.

Format

Here are the elements of screenplay format.

Slug lines: These single-line entries are always capitalized and look like this: EXT. HOUSE—NIGHT.

In a screenplay, a primary slug is placed at the beginning of each scene, flush with the left-hand margin (2″). It always includes three pieces of critical information—interior or exterior (INT. or EXT.); then after two spaces, the location (e.g., house); then after another two spaces, the time of day (e.g., DAY, NIGHT, EVENING, DAWN).

A secondary slug may follow to indicate a specific person or thing the

21

audience will see, e.g., a character who the camera is focused on, or a significant object.

Slugs should fit on one line. At the end of a scene, triple-space to the next slug. (Except with the opening slug which you double-space to after FADE IN.)

Either direction or dialogue must come after a slug. You can't follow a slug with another slug. At the bottom of a page, don't use a slug if you don't have room to put something after it. Go to the next page and write the slug.

When you first mention a character, write his name in full and in caps.

There are special slugs that you may want to use:

SERIES OF SHOTS: This is a way to abbreviate description. For instance, if you wanted to show your heroine's typical morning ritual, you might write it this way:

SERIES OF SHOTS
The following shows our heroine's typical morning ritual.
A) She opens her eyes, yawns tiredly.
B) She stumbles into the bathroom, turns on the shower.
C) Realizing she's running late, as usual, she grabs the first thing she sees in her closet.
D) She gulps down a glass of juice, grabs a piece of toast and munches it as she hurries out.

A series of shots is centered on a theme or action, and has a complete structure all its own—a beginning, middle and end. Typically, it's a series of short shots that quickly move a character through a period of time. The slug SERIES OF SHOTS is usually followed by directions explaining what will be shown. Usually, there's no dialogue here, but there are exceptions to that rule.

A montage can be confused with a series of shots. It includes two or more shots that dissolve into each other to create a specific emotional effect. It doesn't have to focus on a particular character or event, and doesn't have to have a beginning, middle and end structure. Dreams are a common subject for a montage. Often, when a writer wants to show a couple falling in love in a fast way, without spending a lot of time on this, a series of shots will be used. A typical example would show a couple on their first date, then subsequent interaction, culminating in a lovemaking scene, or a proposal.

Dialogue shows what is said and who's saying it. It's written in the mid-

22

dle of the page. Begin with the name of the character, centered and all in caps (only first or last name). Then below that center a parenthetical (a direction to the actor), if you're using one. After that comes the speech, which is single-spaced. Dialogue is almost always brief (more about that later).

Capitalization, abbreviation, dashes and ellipses (three dots) are small but critical details that can add to or detract from your script.

Words written all in caps highlight important information, e.g., the first appearance of a character. AD LIB, which indicates general chatter among characters, should be written in caps. This is often used in party scenes or scenes with groups of people, as in an audience watching a performance. You should also capitalize book and song titles.

The first letter of terms like offscreen, voice-over, background and foreground is capped when used in directions.

When a character is speaking and is interrupted by another character, use a dash. Always leave a space on either side of a dash. When a speaker pauses, use ellipses.

When you read screenplays, you'll notice the word CONTINUED at the top or bottom of many of the pages. When used at the top, it's flush with the left margin and followed by a colon. When used at the bottom, it's flush right, double-spaced from the final direction or dialogue on the page, and put in parentheses (CONTINUED). The guideline for using it is simple. Except for the first page of your script, every page begins with either a slug line or CONTINUED. The slug shows that a new scene is beginning. CONTINUED shows that the previous scene is ongoing. If you get to the bottom of a page, and the scene is going to continue to the next page, use CONTINUED to indicate that the scene isn't finished. When the bottom of a page has CONTINUED, then the top of the next page must have it, also.

Sample Screenplay

Following is part of the first act of my CBS movie, *Borrowed Hearts*. This illustrates most of the formatting issues I've discussed. (There are more camera angles here than you would normally use in a script, because this is the final shooting script.)

By the way, you may or may not choose to begin with FADE IN and end with FADE OUT. Some writers like this traditional opening and closing, while others don't. It's purely a matter of personal preference. But always write THE END when your script is finished, centered, in caps and underlined.

ACT ONE

FADE IN:

EXT. MANSION—NIGHT

Beautiful and stately, surrounded by snow-covered evergreens. Warm lights glow inside. It's everyone's fantasy of what a home should look like.

CREDITS ROLL as the camera dollies toward the house, peeping into a window to see a book-lined den with burgundy leather wing chairs. Snaking around the house, we glimpse a tastefully furnished living room. As the camera slips into the dining room, we get a peek through one of the windows, revealing a long table and sideboard loaded with a full Thanksgiving turkey dinner.

Suddenly, a giant human EYE appears in a window as two porcelain figures of a mother and a little girl, in Victorian dress, are placed into the room.

We CUT BACK to discover we are in—

INT. KATHLEEN'S APT.—LIVING ROOM—NIGHT

—and that what we have seen was a child's model dollhouse, and that all the furniture, books, dishes, etc. were miniature versions of the real thing.

ZOEY RUSSELL, seven, is in the process of putting the roof of the house back on. The dollhouse sits in the living room of a small apartment that is decidedly less upscale. But the modest surroundings are brightened by the paintings of Zoey's mother.

KATHLEEN (O.S.)
(Frantically)
Zoey! Come and help!

Zoey turns and runs into the kitchen—

INT. KATHLEEN'S APT.—KITCHEN—NIGHT—CONTINUOUS

—where there's the warm pandemonium of a Thanksgiving feast in progress. Zoey's mother KATHLEEN, thirtyish, is dressed in faded jeans and a sweater that's seen better days. Her clean-cut beauty has been dulled by constant worry about money and long hours at an unrewarding job. Still, there's something enormously appealing about her.

She's preparing the feast with the help of her friend and co-worker CARLY JELLICOE, fortyish and black, with a your-blues-ain't-nothin'-like-my-blues attitude.

Zoey carries plates, helped by Carly's adolescent son JOE, who's got one ear tuned to the football game on TV, and her slightly younger daughter, SAUNDRA. They bring the plates to an ancient, scarred oak table.

BRIDGET DONOVAN, Kathleen's neighbor, gracefully middle-aged, with the aura of a spiritual den mother, brings out the *raison d'etre*—the turkey. As she sets it down, we MOVE IN CLOSE—a carving knife poises over the turkey, ready to make its first slice—and we go:

INT. SAM'S HOUSE—DINING ROOM—NIGHT—CONTINUOUS

—where the knife continues its cut. Only when we PULL BACK, we're in the impressive dining room in the posh home of SAM FIELD. Gleaming crystal, silver, china, on a polished cherry-wood table that could seat ten. But this evening there's only bachelor Sam—thirtyish and decidedly handsome—and an extremely attractive WOMAN about his age, sitting at opposite ends of the long table. The Thanksgiving feast here puts Kathleen's to shame, but somehow the atmosphere is less inviting.

They're being served by a butler, HAWTHORNE, who's from Little Rock but has the pseudo-English haughtiness that appeals to the Ralph Lauren-English-wanna-be set, and by ANNIE, the maid, who is nervous and unsure of herself.

INT. KATHLEEN'S APT.—DINING ROOM—NIGHT—
CONTINUOUS

Bridget is saying grace, while they all hold hands.

INTERCUT WITH:

INT. SAM'S HOUSE—DINING ROOM—NIGHT

Sam and the woman eat caviar, sip fine wine, and eye each other with growing desire.

BACK TO KATHLEEN'S—

Zoey sneaks a finger into a bowl of marshmallowed candied yams. Kathleen looks at her pointedly. Zoey removes her dripping finger, keeps it protectively high in the air as she resumes the prayer position.

BACK TO SAM'S—

The woman's chair is empty. A quick PAN down the table finds the woman in a new chair—right next to Sam. Dipping a well-manicured finger in the cranberry sauce, she offers it to him.

BACK TO KATHLEEN'S—

—where Zoey, awaiting the signal from Kathleen that prayer is over, dips her finger into her mouth, gleefully licking it, and spreading marshmallow all over her lips. Everyone eagerly begins to fill their plates.

END OPENING CREDITS

DISSOLVE THROUGH TO:

Monday morning, following the Thanksgiving weekend.

EXT. KATHLEEN'S APT.—FRONT—MORNING

A rundown, two-story duplex, one up, one down, in a lower-middle-class neighborhood.

Kathleen hurries out, gets into a battered old VW Bug.

PART TWO

Writing Your Screenplay

5 Theme

Most of the time, the biggest difference between a great film and a mediocre one is the depth of the theme. Matt Damon and Ben Affleck won an Oscar for co-writing *Good Will Hunting*. The movie was a huge commercial and critical success, and audiences loved it. The next film Matt Damon did, *Rounders*, failed both critically and commercially. Very few people liked it, let alone loved it. Both films were superficially similar in terms of the character played by Damon and the type of plot. *The difference lay in the theme*. *Good Will Hunting* had the powerful and ultimately inspiring theme of finding a sense of value, in spite of a background of rejection, failure and violence. The theme of *Rounders* seemed to be, "Be who you are, even if that's not a particularly healthy or happy person." Needless to say, that theme didn't resonate with an audience.

The theme of your screenplay is the deepest expression of who you are and what you value. It's *why* you want to tell this story. It can be a message, such as anti-Semitism is wrong (*Gentleman's Agreement*), or simply a deeply felt emotion, such as obsessive love (*Fatal Attraction*).

Another way of defining theme is to say it's the emotional message an audience gets from a movie. While as the writer you must have a strong emotional feeling about the theme, you must also be analytical and objective in expressing it. Theme is a conscious, not unconscious, statement of the intent of the writer. Be clear about the theme of your movie, in order to write the story in a way that will best express it. A simple way of doing this is to ask yourself, "What am I trying to say in this story?" Then figure out how best to say it. Which characters and plot developments will most vividly reflect that theme?

For instance, if your theme is "racism is wrong," you will want to show the negative consequences of bigotry in your story. You certainly won't want to have a character who triumphs in spite of his racist attitudes. Instead, you might want to have a character who's a "skinhead," who realizes that what he's doing is wrong, and who turns his back on his racist connections, perhaps even courageously speaking out in favor of racial tolerance, even though that puts him at risk.

Age Appropriate

In Viki King's inspiring and insightful book *How to Write a Movie in 21 Days*, she discusses the relationship of a writer's age to theme. It is possible for any writer, of any age, to write about any story. You don't have to be a teenager to write a *She's All That* story or a senior citizen to write a *Driving Miss Daisy* story. But it is true that we often tend to focus on certain life themes at certain ages. Ms. King calls these "writes of passage."

If you're struggling to come up with a compelling theme to launch a screenplay, try looking at where you are in your life at this moment. In a very real sense, your hero or heroine is you. The central life issues you're dealing with will probably be the thematic issues you can write most powerfully and knowledgably about.

If you're a teenager, you're probably dealing with a lot of "firsts"—first love, first heartbreak, first sexual experience, first tentative steps as an independent person. Coming-of-age stories are particularly strong with this age group (*Risky Business*).

In your twenties, you may be struggling to establish yourself out in the big wide world. You're starting a career, figuring out what kind of life you want to lead, and choosing beliefs that weren't necessarily passed on to you by your family (*Wall Street*). This tends to be a very idealistic age, with a fervent desire to right wrongs.

In your thirties you may have become mature and independent enough to finally deal with unresolved family issues, especially with your parents (*One True Thing*). This is often when people surpass their parents' achievements and must deal with the mixed emotions of doing so. The thirtieth birthday itself is often a major life turning point, a time when you feel the need to prove yourself or make your dreams come true. This is also a time of exploring mature themes of love, as opposed to adolescent fantasies.

Forty is one of the biggest birthdays of all, fraught with emotional baggage. In your forties, you realize you don't have all the time in the world. It's now or never to make your life what you want it to be, before it's too late. For women, especially, it can be a time of coming into their power, defining themselves as individuals, and not simply as someone's daughter, wife or mother (*The First Wives Club*).

Fifty is midlife, and often a time of new beginnings. The old life dies or changes in some significant way, and major challenges must be met if you're to feel fulfilled, as opposed to bitter and disappointed. Often a character in this age range will deal with a theme of starting over (*Shirley Valentine*).

From the fifties on, the themes are ones of true maturity and wisdom, and perhaps getting your emotional house in order while there is still time to do so (*To Dance With the White Dog*).

Mars and Venus in Screenwriting

There can be a difference between the way a male writer and a female writer approach theme. While there are certainly exceptions to this rule, generally speaking women are drawn to themes of wholeness and connection, whereas men are drawn to themes of proving themselves through a test of some sort.

This certainly doesn't mean that a female writer can't write a screenplay whose theme involves putting the protagonist through a critical test. (Ironically, one of the hottest action screenwriters in Hollywood today is a fifty-year-old woman!) And it doesn't mean that men can't write stories about connection and community. (A male writer wrote *Steel Magnolias*.)

I got so tired of being stereotyped as a "soft, female" writer, that I wrote an extremely edgy, highly erotic screenplay called *Perfect Blonde*. The response to it was what I hoped for—people realized that I could write a broader range of material.

Universal Themes

Most commercially and/or critically successful movies have themes with universal appeal. There's something deeper than the plot that touches an audience's heart and mind. The audience identifies with the characters or situations, usually because most people have had that same experience or wish they could have it.

A common universal theme is "the underdog triumphs" (*Rocky*). Another is revenge (*Payback*). Most people have been wronged in some way, but haven't been able to avenge that wrongdoing. When they see a character onscreen get revenge, they participate vicariously in the satisfaction of seeing the bad guys get their comeuppance.

Perhaps the most dramatically powerful theme is that of "triumph of the human spirit." This is seen in such brilliant films as *Schindler's List* and

Saving Private Ryan. We want to believe that despite whatever obstacles or even tragedies we may face, that somehow our spirit will not only endure but prevail. These films remind us that most people are made of better stuff than we sometimes think as we watch the TV news or look at the darker side of life.

Other strong themes are integrity (*A Man for All Seasons*), redemption (*The Verdict*), or resolution and closure (*The Trip to Bountiful*).

All these themes concern profound human emotions or life passages. The critical factor in determining a theme for your screenplay is choosing one with which you feel the deepest resonance. If you feel a strong connection with a particular theme, and you express it in your story, an audience will feel the same connection.

6 Synopsis/ Treatment

A treatment, which is another word for synopsis, is the backbone of your screenplay. It's your blueprint, just like the blueprint a builder follows in building a house. It keeps you focused and prevents you from wandering off the spine of the story. Simply put, a treatment is a narrative account of your story, written in present tense. For example, a treatment might begin: "A teenage boy in a battered old car pulls up to the curb at a middle-class, suburban house. He leaps out, races to the front door, and desperately pounds on it, screaming, 'Jody, it's me! Let me in!' A beat, then a rather plain teenage girl throws open the door and stares in shock at the boy." Notice that it's important to put as much emotion and sense of action into a treatment as possible. It should be a concise but entertaining read, especially if someone is going to read it before looking at your script.

Aside from coming up with a very good, very commercial idea in the first place, the treatment is the hardest part of the writing process. In it, you lay out the story—the plot and the characters and their arcs. Of the total creative effort involved in completing a screenplay, roughly 75 percent or more goes into working out the story. Who are the main characters? What do they want? Why do they want it? How do they set about accomplishing their goals? What stops them? What are the consequences of their success or failure?

There is a famous story about Agatha Christie, the most successful mystery writer of all time, many of whose books were made into movies. She was walking in her garden with a friend, deep in thought. Suddenly, she exclaimed, "I've just finished my new book!" Her friend asked, "May I read it?" Ms. Christie replied, "Oh, I haven't written it yet." She had simply done the hardest part—figuring out how the story would play out.

Before you can get to where Dame Agatha was at the end of that walk in the garden, you must first determine what kind of movie you want your story to fit into. You've written a logline, encapsulating the essence of your story. But what approach do you want to take? Is this a serious drama? A broad comedy? A romance? The same idea can be developed in any of those genres. For instance, the teen movie *Clueless* was a young, hip romantic comedy take on Jane Austen's classic English novel, *Emma*. Same story, very different approach.

Once you've got your logline and genre, you may still be a little confused as to which aspect of the story to focus on. For instance, in *Witness*, we had many choices. We could have focused the story on police corruption, the relationship between the two cops who were partners, the interaction of the Amish with the outer world, the religious beliefs of the Amish or any number of other things. But from the inception of the idea, I wanted this to be a romantic story. I felt that the wide gulf between the Amish and the outside world provided a perfect barrier to keep two people who love each other from getting together. Because it's so hard to come up with a fresh conflict in a love story, that was too good a dramatic opportunity to pass up.

Deciding to make it a love story determined the form of the movie. It meant the plot would focus on the developing relationship between the hero and heroine. And the subplot, of course, concerned the heroine's son who witnesses a murder.

If you give ten different writers the same logline, they will come up with ten different approaches to the story. Each will bring his own feelings, interests and unique perspective to it. A concept that strikes one writer as a perfect vehicle for hilarious comedy appears to another to be ripe for development as a serious drama.

Fatal Flaws

In doing a treatment, you have an opportunity to find out what's wrong with your story before you actually write the screenplay. You'll be able to tell if you've made the following fatal errors that can prevent even an interesting script from selling:

- A slow setup that doesn't capture the audience's attention quickly enough.
- A confusing beginning that doesn't make it clear to the audience what kind of movie this is, who the protagonist is and what's at stake.
- A sagging middle—a boring Act Two that doesn't have enough twists and turns, barriers and complications, to hold the audience's interest.
- An abrupt ending that feels as if the writer simply got tired of the story and wrapped it up in a hurry.

- A cliched story that has nothing new or fresh about it. This is the "we've seen it before" syndrome.
- Too many intrusive flashbacks that keep stopping the momentum of the story.
- A reliance on voice-overs to get across information, instead of finding a way to show this information through action or dialogue. Show don't tell.
- Too many warring elements. The writer has thrown in everything he can think of in an effort to make the story exciting. Because so much is going on, none of it is very well developed.
- A reliance on lengthy dialogue, as opposed to action or visual elements.

In a treatment you structure the plot and develop the characters of your movie. Structure determines what happens and when it happens. It is defined by the protagonist's goal. It begins with the initial setup, where you establish the main characters, what the movie's about and what's at stake. It moves on to the inciting incident, which launches the real story. The protagonist finds himself in a new situation, with a change of plans. He makes progress toward his goal, despite serious obstacles and complications. Approximately halfway through the movie, the stakes are raised—more is at stake than the protagonist originally conceived. There is a major setback (the "all is lost" moment), followed by renewed determination by the protagonist to achieve his goal. His efforts culminate in the climax, where he succeeds or fails. At the end there's a very brief resolution.

In your treatment, you should know key things about your main characters, especially the protagonist. Usually the protagonist has a wound (either inner or outer), that is an unresolved source of deep pain, and generally precedes the events of the movie. For instance, in *Message in a Bottle* (based on the best-selling novel by Nicholas Sparks), Kevin Costner is mourning the loss of his beloved wife, who died two years before the movie opens. His attachment to her prevents him from fully accepting the love offered by Robin Wright Penn.

The protagonist in any movie must deal with a deep emotional fear. His inner conflict stems from the fact that this fear is an obstacle to fulfillment. Unless the protagonist can resolve this fear, he won't achieve his goal.

A good treatment usually will resemble the following structure.

Act One: This begins with a strong establishing scene, preferably a

35

"hook" that immediately captures the audience's interest. The hero or heroine is introduced in an interesting way, as is the villain or antagonistic force (for instance, tornadoes in *Twister*). The problem is set before the hero, who accepts the challenge, often with serious reluctance or misgivings.

Act Two: This is the backstory explaining the hero's background or the events preceding the beginning of the movie. The hero is in some way attacked or challenged. There are scenes developing the subplot and dealing with the theme. In a romantic story, there will be romantic interludes. The hero will come up against the villain, and at the end of the act, the hero will appear to be defeated, his goal out of reach.

Act Three: The first part of this act is preparation of the plan the hero has come up with to save the day. The middle part of the act is implementing that plan. And the final part of the act is the climax, the ultimate confrontation between hero and villain, followed by a brief resolution scene.

In working on a treatment, a great place to begin is with the ending. Until you know the ending, you can't write your script. (Some writers disagree with this, and love to discover how the story will play out as they write it. Exceptionally talented or very experienced writers will find this easier to do than will novice writers.) Everything in your movie should lead up to the ending.

In general, Act One should have six to ten scenes to set up the main characters and establish what the story is about. Act Two should be approximately fifteen to thirty scenes, focusing on character development, and introducing complications that create barriers to the protagonist achieving his goal. And Act Three should have anywhere from three to ten scenes that show the climax of the story, and a brief epilogue that in some way suggests the future of the protagonist.

The Step Outline

A good way to begin a treatment is with a step outline. This is a scene outline that describes step by step what happens in each scene in just a sentence or two. It shows the order of the scenes and the action that happens in each one. The step outline points toward the direction of your screenplay and helps you decide which sequence, or order of scenes, will be the most dramatic.

Writers commonly use several ways to do a step outline. One is to write a description of each scene on a 3 × 5 or 5 × 7 card, then lay out the cards in order (perhaps pinning them to a bulletin board). Many writers like to do this because it's easy to move the cards around and change scenes from one act to another. Some writers even use different colored cards for each scene.

Another way is to list the scenes in sequential order on a legal tablet, numbering them as you go. Or you may take a large sheet of paper, divide it into three separate sections, and briefly outline the scenes to go in each section.

Remember that every scene you include must relate to the spine of the story. Scenes that are not absolutely necessary shouldn't be included. If you're confused about whether or not a scene is necessary, ask yourself two questions: Does the scene contribute to the development of the character? Does it move the story forward? If the answer to both these questions is "no," then the scene should be thrown out. Doing this will ensure that you have a fast-paced, tightly constructed story.

Also, scenes should be organized in a rising sequence, with each scene heightening the tension of the story.

Whatever method you choose is purely a matter of personal choice. The purpose of all these methods is to help you create the best structure for your screenplay, with each scene moving in a cause-and-effect manner toward an exciting and fulfilling climax.

The Treatment

Once you've done a step outline, you're ready to write the actual treatment, a detailed narrative account of your story. The only hard and fast rules about treatments are that they should be double-spaced and written in present tense. The length is flexible, but nowadays, short treatments, between five to ten pages, are considered best. A good, thorough treatment could almost be shot as a movie. All it's lacking is dialogue.

If you're writing the treatment for yourself, and not as a sales tool to show to a prospective buyer, it isn't essential to write it in an exciting and colorful style. But if you're going to show it to a producer or studio or network executive, approach it as if you're writing the Great American Short Story. It should be vivid and emotional, and not only hold the reader's interest but get her excited about the movie that could be made from it. Use strong prose, by having highly descriptive passages and active as opposed to passive verbs. For example, don't describe your protagonist as poorly dressed; say his clothes hang in filthy tatters.

Don't forget to write visually. Picture each scene in your mind as if you're seeing it on a movie screen.

After you've written your treatment, ask yourself the following questions.

- Does your main character change his basic approach to dealing with the problem at the heart of the story? (Example: the Humphrey Bogart character in *Casablanca*, who goes from determined noninvolvement to passionate partisanship.)
- Or (which is more rare), does your main character remain steadfast in the face of overwhelming problems? (Example: the Harrison Ford character in *The Fugitive*.)
- Does he grow by losing a negative character trait and/or gaining a positive one? (Example: Robert De Niro becoming less focused on appearing macho and more in touch with his emotions in *Analyze This*.)
- Does your hero or heroine resolve his personal problems? (Example: Robin Williams, who combats his suicidal depression by helping people in *Patch Adams*.)
- Does your protagonist achieve the story goal (which happens in most commercial films)?
- Or, does your protagonist fail in achieving the goal, but accomplish something worthwhile nonetheless (which happens in many "tearjerkers," like *Stepmom*)?

Still unsure about what a treatment should look like? The following is a treatment for a family film written with my frequent collaborator, Madeline DiMaggio.

The Challenge

JED COLLINS is a handicapped twelve-year-old. SUNNY is a female Golden Labrador who's been trained to help the disabled. Their unforgettable journey begins when the chartered amphibious plane taking them to visit Jed's grandfather crashes in the Alaska wilderness. To survive, they must struggle against the rugged terrain, wild animals, the weather and even a human predator. Using the knowledge his grandfather taught him, and with Sunny's help, Jed is able to overcome daunting physical challenges. Along the way, he comes to terms with the challenge of his disability, and learns that it was only his belief in his own limitations that kept him down.

The pilot has died in the crash, but Jed and Sunny survive relatively unharmed. As Jed waits for help, Sunny remains obediently at his side, even though Jed wants nothing to do with her. The dog, a recent gift from Jed's parents, is a painful reminder to Jed of his dependency. Before a roller-blading accident seriously injured him, Jed was an energetic, athletic adolescent, the star first baseman on his school baseball team, and an avid hiker and camper with his grandfather, who taught him about nature and surviving in the wilderness. Now, Jed must wear heavy leg braces, and has only limited use of his hands and arms.

He has rejected Sunny, for she embodies his sense of helplessness and what he sees as the bleakness of his future. Now, Jed must learn to not only accept her help, but rely on her, as they battle the forces of nature for their very survival. Neither can prevail without the other. They are each other's only way out. Jed discovers that Sunny is more than just an animal trained to help compensate for his handicap. She is a kindred spirit.

After a couple of lonely, terrifying days waiting to be rescued, Jed realizes he'll either starve to death or freeze before too long. It's fall, and the first heavy storm of the season could come at any time. The meager supplies of food and camping equipment Jed was able to salvage from the wrecked plane won't be enough to help him survive a storm.

Scared to death, but realizing he has no choice, Jed sets out to walk to his grandfather's cabin, about fifty miles away. He knows the right direction—but he also knows how rugged the terrain is, and the dangers he faces, alone in the wilderness, with only Sunny for protection.

Meanwhile, Jed's parents have flown to his grandfather's cabin to be closer to the search for their son. It becomes a race against time, as the weather report shows a big snowstorm approaching. There's no way the boy could possibly survive such a storm.

On the first day, Jed covers only a few miles. His legs are stiff from the cold, and his braces difficult to maneuver. He reaches the top of an icy incline and collapses, grasping a shrub to keep from sliding. Sunny grabs the end of a rope hanging from Jed's waist, and begins to tug. Jed angrily yanks it back, and they begin a humorous tug of war. He yells at her that this is no time to play, but Sunny whines and persists until Jed finally realizes what she's trying to do. Jed takes an end of rope in each hand, and Sunny pulls the slack, which forms a giant loop. With the rope in her mouth, she pulls Jed safely down the treacherous hill on his stomach.

That night, both boy and dog are exhausted. Sunny brings wood so Jed can build a fire. Later, Jed sleeps, but Sunny stands sentinel. She watches over the boy as the embers die out, never taking her eyes off the darkness. Curious wolves come to stare at the boy and the dog. In their eye contact with Sunny is a subtle but powerful invitation to join them in their freedom. But she remains loyal to Jed. At dawn, she curls up next to him to sleep.

The next day they must cross a glacier. Sunny stops, sensing danger, her ears perked to attention. Suddenly the ice begins to crack. She pulls Jed to safety just as the floor of ice beneath them crumbles, revealing a deep crevasse.

When they come to a wide river, it looks as though they've reached an impasse. Not only is the river itself a seemingly insurmountable barrier, but there is a huge grizzly there, feasting on the spawning salmon. Jed finds a canoe that has washed ashore, but there's no oar. He uses a piece of driftwood as a substitute. But as he's getting into the canoe, the grizzly threatens him. Sunny barks at the bear, distracting it long enough for Jed to get into the canoe and push away from shore. Then Sunny dives into the water and paddles over to him. As they cross the river, Jed loses the driftwood oar and Sunny jumps overboard to retrieve it.

Finally, boy and dog face their most deadly adversary—a crazed trapper involved in illegal trapping, who is afraid Jed will turn him into the authorities. When Jed risks his life to save Sunny from the trapper, the bonding of boy and dog is complete. Sunny has suffered a serious injury to one leg from a vicious trap. Jed bandages her leg, then fashions a makeshift travois. He promises Sunny that if she'll just hang in there, he'll get them to safety.

His newfound love for Sunny inspires him to go that extra mile—beyond the limitatioins of his physical handicap—that ends up saving both of them. Pulling Sunny on the travois, Jed finally gets them both near to his grandfather's cabin, where the search party finds them. They have a tearful, joyous reunion with his family.

Along the way on this remarkable journey, Jed learns that he can do a great deal more than he thought he could. If he could survive this ordeal, he can survive anything. And he isn't alone in the challenges he faces. He has Sunny.

<u>THE END</u>

This is obviously a simple, G-rated movie, aimed at a young audience. But it's an adventurous, fast-paced and emotionally compelling story. The hero, Jed, is transformed by his experience. His character arc is clear—he goes from being a boy who feels hopeless because of his handicap, to a boy who has come to terms with his situation and proven to himself that there's nothing he can't do. The plot builds in intensity, with ever greater dangers threatening boy and dog, climaxing in the greatest danger of all, the villainous trapper.

Unfortunately, this story didn't sell because there were simply too many movies at that time about children lost in the wilderness. But if it had sold, it would have been relatively simple to write the screenplay, because the treatment was so well worked out.

7 Characterization

Creating compelling characters is the key to attracting the stars who get both feature films and television movies made. *Witness* got made when a bankable star, Harrison Ford, decided he wanted to play the lead character. *Borrowed Hearts* was made when a bankable TV star, Roma Downey, decided she wanted to play the heroine. Even in low-budget, independent movies, there are lists of bankable actors and actresses.

If you look at the vast majority of movies that get made, almost all have either bankable actors or hot newcomers. The only exceptions are movies whose concept is so strong, either because it's sexy (*sex, lies, and videotape*) or big (*Jurassic Park*), that audiences are drawn in despite the lack of stars.

Producer Laura Ziskin, quoted earlier about the importance of casting, went on to say, "I think bankability is important. [But there is] the example of this movie we're doing, *A Cool, Dry Place*. The central character was a guy in his midtwenties. That's a castable movie. We happen to have cast somebody who we think is on the rise, who isn't a movie star. Did we start out saying, 'Wouldn't this movie be great for Tom Cruise?' Yeah. But we knew Tom Cruise wasn't going to do the movie. I guess what I'm saying is that if it's a one-armed, sixty-year-old man, I've got limited choices . . . I don't want to spend my time on something where I get down the road and I say, 'God, this is really good but there's nobody who can play it.' "

Characters are also what an audience remembers best about movies. Most people can't recall the details of plots, but they can remember the characters. Whether it's Jack Nicholson playing a neurotic and rude curmudgeon in *As Good As It Gets* or Robert Duvall as a messianic preacher in *The Apostle*, the characters remain indelibly etched in our memories.

So how do you create the kind of characters actors will want to play and audiences will remember? The key is knowing your characters as well as you know your family members, your best friends—even yourself. Characters must seem real to you, must "come alive" in your mind before they can come alive onscreen. You make a character come alive by knowing the following things about him:

- His full name, including nickname, if any.
- His exact age and birthdate.
- His ethnicity and cultural/religious heritage. You don't have to belong to a particular ethnic group to write about that group, though it certainly helps. But if you're writing about a group that you don't belong to—for instance, when I wrote about the Amish in *Witness*—do your homework. It isn't simply a matter of thorough research. You must try to understand the world of your story from the character's point of view. Above all, avoid stereotypes. They are inherently demeaning.
- Physical appearance, including hair and eye color, height, weight, etc. (Make some part of his appearance *actable*, e.g., a certain movement, a particular walk, a shy smile.)
- Marital status.
- Birthplace.
- Familial relationships—parents, siblings, extended family or lack thereof.
- Educational background.
- Job.
- Political/social beliefs.
- Morality/ethics/values. This can be an opportunity for you, the writer, to express your own deeply held convictions. Many of the best films express the belief that some values are worth fighting and dying for (*Saving Private Ryan*). And often films deal with characters in crisis who must make moral choices and examine their values. Characters don't have to talk about their values. They can show them through their actions or attitudes.
- Personality traits, both positive and negative.
- Significant mannerisms, use of language, speech patterns.
- Financial status/social class.
- First love.
- Best friends.
- Worst enemies.
- Greatest fear. Knowing your protagonist's greatest fear is the most important element of all. More about that later.

Writing a character study, or biography, and thus knowing your character's back story, is a good beginning, but there's much more involved in it than that.

Defining Moment

One of the most insightful lessons I ever learned about characterization is this: There is a defining moment in everyone's life, usually when we are young, and often involving our family, that defines us for the rest of our lives. We may keep going back to this, in one way or another, trying to redo it and make it turn out better. We subconsciously design our lives to keep playing this out over and over again. An example would be a woman who becomes sexually involved with many men in a desperate attempt to find the love and approval she didn't receive from an absent or critical father. (The Bill Murray comedy, *Groundhog Day*, is a perfect example of this concept of repeating something until we get it right.)

Figuring out a compelling defining moment in your main character's life will give that character direction, and that will create plot. Character is action. Ask yourself how that moment defined what the character wants. Because the basic question of any movie is, what does the protagonist want and what will he do to get it?

Sometimes the answer to this question is simple. In *Payback*, Mel Gibson's character wants the $70,000 stolen from him. More often, the character thinks he wants one thing, but during the course of the movie will discover that he wants something much deeper and more important. In *Shakespeare in Love*, the title character thinks he just wants inspiration to overcome his writer's block. But by the end of the movie, he's fallen in love with his muse and wants her much more than he wants success as a playwright.

You don't necessarily have to explain in your script what the defining moment was for your character. But you, the writer, must know it. In *Witness*, it is never spelled out for the audience where the detective-hero's rigid sense of right and wrong comes from. But as the writer, I knew it was a result of being deeply disappointed in the people most important to him, his parents. Therefore, he held everyone, including himself, to an impossibly high standard, which isolated him from people.

Having your protagonist reveal his defining moment can be extremely effective. Perhaps the most touching scene in *Borrowed Hearts* is when the hero confides in the little girl that when he was young he was rejected by his father because he couldn't play sports well. That was very important to his father, who had been a star athlete. That rejection made the hero emotionally closed off and driven to succeed in order to prove his father wrong.

This defining moment applies to all genres, from the broadest comedy to the most serious drama. In *The Wedding Singer*, Adam Sandler's defining moment was when he was a child and his parents died. This made him desperate to get married and have the security of having a family. So when his worst nightmare happens and his fiancée stands him up at the altar, he goes into a deep but comical depression.

The best way to play out your character's defining moment is to have him face his worst fear that is connected to it. In Hitchcock's classic suspense film, *Vertigo*, Jimmy Stewart's defining moment is when he helplessly witnesses someone fall to his death. This creates his pathological fear of heights. Later, he must confront that fear to save the woman he loves.

The defining moment should create your character's biggest flaw or weakness. When the character is forced to confront the repercussions of that defining moment, he has an opportunity to finally overcome it.

By the way, the antagonist, or villain, should be the person or force who is in the best position to take advantage of your protagonist's weakness or flaw. For instance, in *Twister*, Helen Hunt's defining moment occurred when she was a little girl and saw her father killed by a tornado. As an adult, she must confront the resulting fear of tornadoes.

Do not reveal a character's entire back story in one fell swoop. Scatter the information throughout the script, on a need-to-know basis. Tell us only what we need to know at the time we need to know it. Monologues, flashbacks and factual exposition can be terribly boring, and can stop the momentum of the story. Back story should come out a little bit at a time, in brief exchanges of dialogue, rather than lengthy speeches. And never forget that the sole purpose of back story is to motivate your character in the "front" story.

Four Aspects of Character

There are four things your main characters—hero, heroine and villain or antagonist—must have:

1. A clearly defined need or goal.
2. A strong conflict involved in meeting that need or achieving that goal.
3. A plan of action.
4. A resolution to both the inner and outer conflict the character feels.

In *Witness,* the hero has a goal—catching a killer. The conflict he faces in reaching that goal is twofold: the discovery that the killer is a fellow policeman and that the hero's own boss and friend is involved. His plan is to get the witness to the killing, a vulnerable child (and his mother) to safety, then figure out a way to circumvent the official corruption. At the end of the movie, the hero has resolved the outer conflict—the murder case—and the inner conflict—his love for a woman he cannot have.

In this movie, the heroine has a goal—protecting her child who is in danger because he witnessed a murder. Her conflict in achieving that goal revolves around the fact that she must bring an outsider into the closed Amish community. Her plan is to disguise this outsider by dressing him in Amish garb, so the villain can't find them. At the end, her outer conflict—the cultural gulf between herself and the hero—has been resolved. Her inner conflict—her love for him, which is prohibited by her culture, has also been resolved via a bittersweet parting.

The villain, a corrupt cop, has a goal—protecting his career and concealing his theft of millions of dollars worth of drugs. He has a profound conflict because he isn't an entirely bad man, just greedy, and to protect himself, he must kill his friend, the hero of the movie. His plan is to find out where the hero is hiding, and kill him. At the end, his outer conflict is resolved when he is captured. His inner conflict is resolved when he connects with the remaining vestiges of decency within his soul and can't bring himself to kill his friend.

There are three other essential ingredients of characterization. A character must:

1. Have a clear point of view, usually expressed in dialogue.
2. Have an attitude expressed in action.
3. Undergo a significant change by the end of the movie.

Point of view and attitude are not the same thing. Point of view is how the character sees the world. Is he conservative or liberal, trusting or cynical, gullible or an opportunist? Attitude is how he expresses his point of view. If he's conservative, his mannerisms, dress and behavior will be quite different than if he's liberal. If his point of view is sexually repressive, he'll behave one way, and if it's uninhibited, he'll behave in a totally different way.

One of the most common "notes" that executives and producers give to writers regarding screenplays is, "Give the character more attitude." A colorful example of attitude was the Fonzie character in the 1970s TV sitcom, *Happy Days*. With his ultrahip persona, dress and mannerisms, he defined "cool" for a generation. By telling a writer to give a character more attitude, what the executive is really saying is, "Make him more vivid. Make him come alive."

Change is the most critical factor in characterization. If your protagonist is the same at the end of your screenplay as he was at the beginning, you've failed. Character growth is essential for most movies. There are rare exceptions; for instance, in a story where the main character remains steadfast, but impacts others around him (*Patton*). But most movies are simply efforts to track the growth and change of the main character.

Values

One of the greatest aspects of creating characters is having an opportunity to express your values through these characters. For instance, this exchange in *Witness* clearly expresses my personal convictions about violence and also the Amish value toward violence.

Rachel, the Amish heroine, comes in after the hero, John Book, a cop, has been showing his gun to Rachel's young son, Samuel, who's fascinated by it.

                    RACHEL
John Book, while you are in this house, I insist that you respect our ways.

                    JOHN
Right. Here. Put it somewhere where it's safe. Where he won't find it.

This scene is followed by one between Samuel and his grandfather, Eli, who expresses the Amish attitude toward weapons of destruction.

                    ELI
The gun—that gun of the hand is for the taking of human life. Would you kill another man?

Samuel stares at it, not meeting his grandfather's eyes. Eli leans forward, extends his hands ceremonially.

> ELI
>
> What you take into your hands, you take into your heart.

A beat, then Samuel musters some defiance.

> SAMUEL
>
> I would only kill a bad man.

> ELI
>
> Only a bad man. I see. And you know these bad men on sight? You are able to look into their hearts and see this badness?

> SAMUEL
>
> I can see what they do. I have *seen* it.

> ELI
>
> And having seen, you would become one of them? So that the one goes into the other into the other, into the other...?

He breaks off, bows his head for a moment. Then he fixes the boy with a stern eye and, driving the heel of his palm firmly into the tabletop, with enormous intensity:

> ELI (contd)
>
> "Wherefore come out from among them and be ye separate, saith the Lord!"
> ELI (contd)
> (indicating pistol, continuing from Corinthians 6:17)
> "And touch not the unclean thing!"

This scene is one of the most meaningful in the entire screenplay because the characters are stating, in a way that is wholly in keeping with the theme of the movie, a deeply held belief of the writers.

Fatal Flaw/Tragic Flaw

Often the most interesting protagonists in movies have a tragic or fatal flaw. The difference is that usually a fatal flaw can and will be overcome; the tragic flaw cannot be overcome, and leads to the destruction of the protagonist. The tragic flaw is inevitable. Usually, the audience recognizes this from early in the movie. The protagonist knows it, or at least senses it, and tries to avoid it, but can't. Thus, tragedy results.

In *Silence of the Lambs*, the heroine, Clarice Starling (played by Jodie Foster) has a fatal flaw that ironically matches the flaw of the villain—both are intensely insecure and lonely. But she is able to understand her flaw and successfully deal with it, unlike the villain. In the end, the villain senses this fatal flaw and tries to use it against her, but fails when she finds enough self-confidence to outwit him.

Very few movies have a protagonist with a tragic flaw, because this is, by definition, a real downer. In these cases, the protagonist fails because he can't overcome his flaw. The classic 1970s film, *Five Easy Pieces*, is a brilliant example. The Jack Nicholson character is a talented but self-destructive man who ends up alone and a failure because he can't overcome the tragic flaw of self-doubt instilled in him as a child by his perfectionist father.

Powerful examples of flaws are blind ambition in *The Candidate*, excessive greed in *Wall Street*, addictive love in *Fatal Attraction* and unresolved rage in *Raging Bull*.

Since writing is often a way of holding up a mirror to ourselves, and the most powerful stories are ones we relate to personally, it's interesting to examine our own psyche for examples of fatal, or even tragic, flaws, then create stories in which to explore them. If you look at how a particular flaw has led you down a certain path that hasn't been productive, or how you've managed to overcome a flaw in order to succeed, you have grist for the writer's mill.

Compelling Villains

By definition, the villain is the bad character who is trying to stop the hero from achieving his goal. He is the antagonist—but not all antagonists are villains. For example, if your hero wants to join the Marines, but isn't quite fit enough to pass the grueling physical requirements, then the recruitment officer might be the antagonist, without being a bad guy.

If you have a story with an actual villain—a truly bad person—then the

49

story automatically becomes about good vs. evil. In these stories, the hero will stand for anything that represents an affirmation of life, while the villain will oppose life. Evil tyrannizes the weak, restricts freedom and rights, is repressive, and belittles, humiliates or destroys others.

You must ask yourself why your villain is doing what he is doing. For many villains, doing harm is a result of themselves being harmed, usually when they were young and/or vulnerable. Societal or personal factors come into play here. Other villains act in response to unconscious factors, such as mental illness. They're unaware of the unconscious forces driving them. They're driven by what psychologists call their "shadow" side, and they strive to justify their actions. All villains are narcissistic. They can't see or respect other people's feelings, needs or reality.

The most interesting villains are convinced they're right. They justify their horrific behavior because of past harm done to them, or else they insist they're doing whatever evil deed they're involved in to honor a greater cause. This cause is so important to them that they insist anything they do in the name of it is OK. If you have a villain behaving without motivation (i.e., "He's just crazy" or "He's just bad"), he will be an uninteresting villain. And since your hero is only as strong as your villain (because he tests himself in confronting him), this will weaken your hero.

Personalizing Characters

When creating characters, especially your protagonist, find some element in the character that is also in you. It's much easier to write about a character who you truly understand because you relate to him. But how can you relate to a villain? By taking a feeling you have (e.g., strong political beliefs) or an experience that impacted you deeply (e.g., being humiliated by a schoolyard bully) and letting your imagination carry it far beyond where you actually allowed it to go in your real life. For instance, you might wish you could have gotten revenge against the bully, even though you would never act on that desire. But your villain can act on it—in a big way. You might strongly oppose a particular politician, but would go no farther than trying to vote him out of office. Your villain, however, could be an assassin, as in *In the Line of Fire*.

If you invest something of yourself in a character and find yourself stuck in writing a scene, ask yourself, "How would I act in this situation?" Or, "How would I feel about this?" That will give you the solution to your problem. In every scene in your screenplay, you must know (and show) how every character in that scene feels and why he's behaving the way he is.

Don't assume an actor will give your character the qualities you haven't given him in the screenplay. Unless there's something interesting on the page for an actor to play, he won't want to do that role. Actors do bring a great deal to characters (Harrison Ford improvised on the set my favorite scene in *Witness*—the dance scene in the barn). But the writer must first create a wonderful character who is as fully fleshed out as possible.

A great way to create multidimensional characters who are complex and fascinating, is to give them warring elements within themselves. Establish a primary quality, such as stinginess, then ask what quality would create conflict with that, for instance, a penny-pinching person who is forced to give away a great sum of money to achieve his goal.

Ask yourself the following questions about your main characters.

- Have I shown his most important qualities through action or dialogue?
- What makes him interesting? Compelling? Fascinating? Different? Unpredictable?
- Does he sometimes do the unexpected, or is he boringly predictable?
- Is it clear how he feels?
- Why does he react the way he does?
- Why does he want what he wants?
- What event in his back story defines him? (Specific events in the past create specific character traits in the present.)
- How did he react internally to important events in his past, especially his childhood? Early adolescence—around eleven, twelve or thirteen—is a particularly interesting time to explore. (Every adult has a child of the past within him. If you understand this "inner child," you know the driving forces affecting your character.)
- Does every character in my screenplay have a critical function that is absolutely necessary to tell the story or express the theme?
- Are my minor characters refreshingly drawn, or merely stereotypes?
- Do I have characters who strongly contrast with the hero or heroine, and thus add color and texture?

If you can answer all these questions satisfactorily, you'll have wonderful characters who audiences will long remember.

Conceiving a Character

How do you begin? Whether you're basing a character on someone you know well or someone you've merely observed, or you're creating a composite character with qualities taken from different people, giving birth to a character usually begins with one vivid stroke. For instance, here's my initial description of the hero (a Wyoming rancher) in my as-yet-unproduced screenplay *Straight From the Heart*: "Tall and lean and tough as a juniper root, Tyler is cowboy enough to handle just about anything."

Short and to the point. Tyler is a quintessential romantic fantasy.

In another script, *Perfect Blonde*, the title character is introduced thusly: "Jordan—the exquisite face we saw on the computer earlier. With a body to match. She moves with a sinuous grace, completely self-contained, yet aware of her impact on every man there. She's dressed simply, in a bra top and short pencil skirt that shows off her long legs. Her blonde hair is pulled back in a ponytail. If she was a centerfold, she'd be in *Playboy*, not *Penthouse*. She outclasses every other woman in the room. And she's the icon of Matt's desire."

Jordan is, in a sense, what most women would love to be but know they aren't—a femme fatale.

Both Tyler and Jordan are fantasy characters. The heroine of *Borrowed Hearts* is much more realistic and closer to who I am—a hardworking, devoted mom. The little girl, Zoey, in the same movie, is in many ways myself as a child—precocious, vulnerable, eager to please. But both those characters are only partly me. They're mostly made up. I found elements in these characters who were me, without writing autobiographical characters.

How do you create a character? By following these steps:

- Base your character on someone you've observed, a combination of people or on some aspect of yourself.
- Make the first broad brushstroke in describing the character (a blonde bombshell, a rugged cowboy).
- Find the emotional core of the character. Who is he in his most secret heart?
- Make him a paradox in some ways (the tongue-tied hero of *Message in a Bottle*, who can write eloquent, passionate love letters). A character must be consistent and yet, at times, surprising. Human nature being what it is, we all act "out of character" at times. Paradox is the crux of a fascinating character.
- Give him a full range of emotions and attitudes. Feel his pain, his ex-

hilaration, his hopelessness or stubborn determination to succeed despite the odds. In many of the best movies, with the most memorable characters, we empathize with them. We actually feel as if we share failed boxer Rocky Balboa's frustration in the first *Rocky*, or the teenager Conrad's depression in *Ordinary People*.

- Make him specific, not generic. (In *Jerry Maguire*, Tom Cruise didn't play a stereotypical sports agent. He played an agent who is by definition ruthless, but with a deeply conflicted conscience.)

Above all, keep in mind that your initial description of your character must be compelling enough to make an actor want to play him. For instance, the female lead in *Fatal Attraction* could have simply been described as a sexy blonde with an edgy quality. The actual description in the screenplay was: "At that moment, an extremely attractive blond girl passes by . . . She turns and gives him a look to make hell freeze over . . . She really is sensational-looking. She must be in her thirties, but she dresses younger, trendily, and gets away with it."

See the difference?

In describing characters, be general enough so that any number of actors can play the role, but specific enough so that an interesting, concrete character is there. The male leads in many movies are, in a sense, generic heroes. They could be played by any number of actors, each of whom would put his particular stamp on the character. If you create a character who is so narrowly defined that only a small number of actors can play him, and none of those actors are available or interested, then you're in trouble.

Emotions/Attitudes

What is the full range of emotions that a character can play? In simple terms, they're mad, sad, glad and scared.

- Mad—angry, enraged, irritated, frustrated, mildly peeved. See the range of emotions within this one area?
- Sad—depressed, suicidal, discouraged, self-destructive, wistful.
- Glad—brimming over with joy, ecstatic, happy, pleased.
- Scared—terrified, horrified, anxious, fearful.

How do you convey attitudes? Through opinions expressed by the characters or a particular worldview ("People are basically good." "Most

53

people will cheat you as soon as look at you."). Attitudes deepen your character and reveal a great deal about her.

The depth of characterization in a screenplay has been accurately compared to an iceberg. The audience may only see a small percentage of the work that has gone into creating a character, but the writer needs to know the rest of this information to create a deeply drawn character.

Relationships

For me, as for most screenwriters, the most fascinating aspect of creating characters is exploring their relationships. Most movies focus on the interaction between characters who love or hate each other (or both). The chemistry between characters, their interplay, can be as important as how well drawn the characters themselves are.

These relationships can be romantic or nonromantic, but they must nevertheless be interesting. The key to creating a successful relationship in a romantic movie is making it clear to the audience why these two people should be together. The attraction between them must be clear to the audience, even when it isn't clear to the characters. And we should understand why they would be good for each other, so that we care whether or not they get together. Nora Ephron, who has written and/or directed several of the most successful romantic comedies of the last decade (*When Harry Met Sally, Sleepless in Seattle*), has been quoted as saying that the key factor in whether or not a romantic comedy is successful is how sympathetic the hero and heroine are, and how badly the audience wants to see them get together.

The most entertaining relationships to watch onscreen involve characters who have the most conflict. Conflict can come from contrasting qualities (the shy librarian and the fast-talking salesman in *The Music Man*). Opposites truly do attract, especially in movies. These opposite qualities can involve different ambitions, motivations, backgrounds, goals, values or attitudes.

Or it can be a result of conflicting goals (the independent bookstore owner vs. the big-chain-megastore tycoon in *You've Got Mail*). But whatever the source of the conflict, it's imperative that characters have the ability to transform each other. By the end of *Jerry Maguire*, both the hero and heroine have been transformed for the better. She's stronger and he's capable of a truly intimate, committed relationship.

A simple formula to follow, especially in romantic relationship stories is: attraction = conflict = contrast = transformation.

The Eternal Triangle

Triangle stories are among the most dynamic and dramatic. *Fatal Attraction*—husband/wife/mistress—is one highly successful example. There is a strong contrast between the mistress and wife. One is sexually promiscuous and ultimately homicidal; the other is the ultimate example of a devoted wife and mother, protecting her family from a serious threat.

In triangle stories, the lone female or lone male must be forced to make a choice—and it can't be an easy one. Both choices must be appealing in some critical way. The drama will stem from either the difficulty of the choice or the consequences of it. The strongest choices are those that involve a moral in some way. Often, one of the participants in a triangle is acting in response to subconscious, self-destructive impulses (the happily married, basically decent husband deciding to have a "fling" in *Fatal Attraction*).

There is usually something hidden in a triangle story—often it's the lone male or lone female's involvement with the "other person." When this secret is brought into the open, this is known as the "reveal." It inevitably leads to a crisis, followed by the climax of the film.

Supporting Characters

Minor characters in movies must be there for a reason—not just because they're colorful or fun characters. A minor character must be necessary to the telling of the story. He can serve any number of functions: He can help to define the protagonist, express the theme of the movie or help move the story forward. He can be a catalyst, inspiring or forcing the main character to act or react. Or he can convey information that would be awkward or inappropriate for the main character to convey.

Again, as with the relationship between the primary characters, it's often useful to strongly contrast a supporting character with a main character. These can be physical contrasts or attitudinal ones (the rather cowardly, unattractive character Joe Pesci plays in *Lethal Weapon* vs. the heroic and attractive Mel Gibson character).

Often you must rely on "character types" for supporting characters: the devoted mother, rebellious teenager, fast-talking salesman. But that doesn't mean they have to be cliches. You can put a fresh spin on even these jaded types to make them entertaining and interesting.

Following are ways to avoid stereotypes:
- Make characters multidimensional, rather than one-dimensional.
- Don't put characters from a particular group in a narrow, traditional

role (the black maid, Hispanic gang member, etc.).

- Have characters from all ethnic and cultural groups, ages, socioeconomic backgrounds and physical appearance, including the disabled.

Getting Unstuck

All writers face the frustration of dealing with a character who refuses to "come to life," or the confusion of not knowing what a character should do in a particular scene. There are some effective techniques for dealing with these issues. When you're stuck, look at the subconscious goal of the character—what she really wants inside vs. what she says or thinks she wants. This will help you understand the character in a more in-depth manner.

Consider a radical solution: Change the gender of a character. A friend of mine was struggling with a character in a medical thriller. This character was a male doctor and simply wasn't very interesting. I suggested making the doctor a female pediatrician (children played a significant role in the plot). A pregnant female pediatrician. Suddenly the character came to life, and my friend couldn't write fast enough to get down all his thoughts about who this character was and why she was doing what she was doing. He created a wonderful, complex, dynamic, sympathetic character, where before there had been an uninteresting one.

Gender switching can be particularly effective and exciting if you take a traditional male role and turn it into a female role. The character of Ripley in *Alien* was written for a male actor. If that's how it had been cast, it would have been an exciting, but not particularly special, film. When Sigourney Weaver was cast, the character wasn't rewritten, but suddenly the whole tenor of the movie changed for the better. Suddenly it was fresh and unique, not just another sci-fi action thriller.

Perhaps the single most helpful piece of advice I've been given about dealing with being stuck with a character came from a psychologist who's a former screenwriter and whose practice is primarily aimed at writers. He suggested that I take a feeling I'm having—for instance, self-doubt about my ability to successfully execute a difficult project—and give it to my main character. Through that character, write about how it feels—the fear, insecurity, stress. Let that character express those feelings in dialogue, or act on them. As the character explores these feelings and works through them, I can work through them as a writer. In the process, the character will come alive.

8 Structure

Many books on the craft of screenwriting hold up *Witness* as an example of effective structure, and analyze it in detail, looking at what makes it tick. The irony is that in the three years the screenplay was consistently rejected, the most common criticism was its structure. As many people said, "Nothing happens in the second act."

What makes the second act of the movie work, however, is that "structure is character." The main characters determine the events, or structure, of the movie. The second act of *Witness* can be seen as the strongest, most emotionally compelling part of the entire movie, because it focuses on the development of the hero and heroine, and their change and growth through their romantic experience.

Mythic Structure

I'm going to begin this discussion of structure—in many ways the most critical aspect of a screenplay and often the weakest—with a brief overview of the mythic structure. Myths are the timeless stories, passed down for literally thousands of years, that are at the root of our universal existence. A myth is a story that most people, in all cultures and walks of life, feel an emotional connection to, because in some small way they've experienced it. Myths reflect universal themes of struggle and victory, failure and redemption.

In his powerful work *The Hero With a Thousand Faces*, author Joseph Campbell explains the hero myth, breaking it into a step-by-step formula. Most critically or commercially successful films follow this formula. The *Star Wars* movies and the *Indiana Jones* trilogy are prime examples. (Both George Lucas and Steven Spielberg have a particularly strong sense of myth and incorporate it into their movies with tremendous success.) *Witness* is another example. Every time I write a script, I structure it according to this timeless tradition.

The mythic hero's journey has specific story events that reveal the true nature of the hero, enable him to learn what he truly needs for fulfillment, and provide him with the opportunity to be transformed into a better, more heroic, person. This is the structure:

Act One

We meet the hero or heroine in the "ordinary" world.

The hero is confronted by a "call to adventure," a problem or challenge that will change his destiny.

The hero is usually reluctant to accept this call, because of fear of the unknown or of outside forces that appear to be overwhelming. Often a warning to the hero against undertaking the journey is involved in this call. The hero isn't completely committed to the "mission." He has second thoughts, but is nudged or forced into a "state of no return."

Often there is a "wise one," literally a wise old man or woman, a partner (especially in "buddy" pictures), or some kind of cohort who guides the hero. The purpose of this "mentor" is to assist the hero in his transition to the other world. The mentor may provide special tools or knowledge to the hero to aid him on his journey.

Act Two

The hero crosses the first threshold into the "other world." The adventure gets going. This is the first time the hero has made a definite decision to accept the challenge. The turning point from Act One—the setup of the hero's decision to act—and Act Two—which portrays the action itself—is often enacted in terms of traveling to a new place or environment or life circumstance.

On this journey the hero encounters tests of his courage and wisdom and character. New challenges constantly arise, as the hero learns the "rules" of the other world. The hero encounters both favorable and unfavorable consequences of his actions. He meets supporting characters who may serve as allies or a love interest. And he is tested by his main antagonist or lesser enemies.

The hero comes to the second threshold he must cross: a dangerous place known as the "inmost cave." It can be the headquarters of the villain or the arena in which the hero will find the object of his quest. Most importantly, this is the hero's moment of truth. He must confront the innermost fears that hold him back.

The hero goes through the "supreme ordeal." He hits rock-bottom. All appears to be lost. The hero may come close to death. He must seem to die, even if only in a symbolic sense, to be reborn as a stronger, better person. In a love story, this is the boy-loses-girl moment. In an action/adventure story it's literally a life-or-death moment. The hero must confront outer manifestations of what he fears most.

Having barely survived, through his courage and wits, the hero now takes possession of the prize he has been seeking. In a love story, this is where boy-gets-girl, at least for a love scene. But getting this prize doesn't mean the story is over. Now the hero must apply his hard-won wisdom or power before he can travel back to safety.

The road back is perilous. The hero must deal with the consequences of having seized his prize. In action/adventure films, the adversaries spring into action, chasing the hero (the standard final-climactic-action sequence). The hero must confront these adversaries, who want the prize he's taken.

Act Three
The turning point from Act Two to Act Three often involves a resurrection of some kind, a second life-or-death moment when the evil forces are given one last shot at defeating the hero. Because the hero has been transformed by his experience, he triumphs against these forces.

The hero returns to his ordinary life, changed in a significant way.

The hero brings back something—the original prize he sought, or something unexpected and even more valuable. Because he possesses this, the ordinary world as he once knew it has changed.

A variation on the hero myth focuses on "healing." In this type of story, the protagonist is ill or "broken" and must embark on a physical or emotional journey in order to heal. Being "broken" can be physical, psychological or emotional. In "healing," the main character not only becomes whole, but experiences love as well. In fact, in these stories, love is usually both the healing force and the reward the protagonist wins at the end. *Witness* is an example of both a hero myth and a healing myth.

Overview of Structure
Here is a brief delineation of structure.

- Begin with an image that reflects the style, mood and theme of the story. (The waving grain, connoting sustenance and basic values, in

Witness. The charming dollhouse, representing the security of home and family, in *Borrowed Hearts*.)

- A strong, dramatic or comedic event or catalyst captures the audience's attention and gets the story going.
- A "central question" is clearly defined. (In *Witness*, will John Book catch the killer? In *Borrowed Hearts*, will the little girl get a father?)
- The first turning point, from Act One into Act Two, brings up the central question, reveals more about the true character of the protagonist, changes the direction of the story and sets up the nature of the conflict between the protagonist and antagonist. It leads the action into Act Two.
- The second turning point brings up the central question again, raises the stakes (by keeping the hero's goal out of reach or adding something new at stake) and builds to an action crisis that leads to a realization by the protagonist that automatically sets up the climax.
- The climax is a big finish, completely satisfying to the audience, whether it's happy, bittersweet or tragic. The hero has begun as one kind of person and been transformed in a fundamental way. The plot is a direct reflection of this transformation.
- Ending with a quick resolution that ties up any loose ends of the plot and suggests the future of the protagonist.

Another way of looking at structure is this:

Act One is all about *who*: Who is the main character? The audience must fall in love with him, or at least find him fascinating, even if he's a deeply flawed protagonist (Jack Nicholson in *As Good As It Gets*).

Act Two is all about *what*: What must he do to achieve his goal, and what happens to change him?

Act Three is all about *how*: How does he overcome the final obstacle, solve his problem or reach his goal, and triumph (or not)?

That, briefly, is the most commonly used structure in commercial films.

There are, of course, other types of structure. A few of the most acclaimed movies do not follow this structure (*Pulp Fiction*). In most action movies, or high-concept comedies, there is a major action or comedic scene or sequence every ten minutes or so. This keeps up the pace essential to the success of those movies. In independent films, and occasionally in major studio releases, the structure may be nonlinear (*Out of Sight*).

Almost from the very beginning of drama, stories have fallen into the three-act structure. Whether it's a feature film, TV movie (artificially divided into seven acts to accommodate commercial breaks), half-hour sitcom (divided into two acts to accommodate commercials) or hour drama episode (divided into four acts for the same purpose), the stories almost always fall into this pattern of beginning, middle and end—setup, development, resolution.

While these figures are not carved in stone, acts will generally fall along these lines: roughly twenty pages of setup in Act One; forty-five to sixty pages of development in Act Two; and a fast-paced twenty to thirty pages in Act Three; followed by an extremely brief (no more than five minutes or so) resolution.

Moving from one act to another usually involves a clearly defined turning point. Because the line of action should continually rise to ever greater heights of drama or comedy, graphing the three-act structure would look like this:

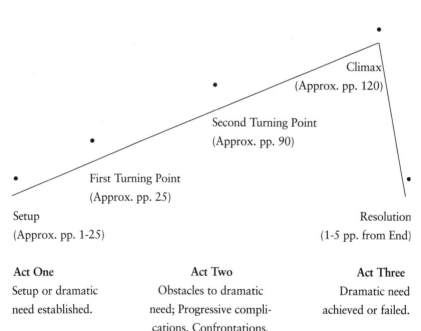

Each act has a specific purpose and pace. The first act should get moving as quickly as possible, the second act may have a slower (but not sluggish) momentum, and the last act should have the fastest pace of all, as the action builds in urgency and intensity.

The Setup

The setup should only include information vital to getting the story started. Who are the main characters? What kind of story is it? What is the spine or direction of the story?

Most good movies begin with an opening image that reflects the place, time, mood and sometimes theme of the story. It has been said that often audiences will make up their minds as to whether or not they're going to like a movie in the opening minute. I believe that's true. If you find it hard to believe, as I did when I first heard it, try this little test. The next time you go to a movie, wait till the first minute or so is over, then ask yourself if you feel positively or negatively disposed toward the movie. Is your interest piqued, or do you already feel the first faint stirrings of disappointment? Then at the end of the movie, ask yourself if that initial response was accurate or not. You'll be surprised how often it is.

Often, the opening of a movie has little or no dialogue and is visually oriented. Here's what we see in the first three minutes of *Witness*:

A lyrical image of grain blowing in the wind. (The Director of Photography, John Seale, received a well-deserved Academy Award nomination.)

Several Amish, dressed in traditional black clothing, walking through the waving grain.

Amish carriages moving down the road.

A farmhouse.

A somber funeral.

Faces of n.d. (nondescript) Amish.

The first dialogue we hear is German (Pennsylvania Dutch are actually of German descent). This adds to the general feeling on the part of the audience of "What's going on here?"

The opening rhythm of the movie is slow and deliberate. We are introduced to a peaceful, close-knit community. These people are close to the land. The pace of life here is much slower and more peaceful than in a city. They are connected to the earth and to their community.

The theme is clearly established: community. As the movie proceeds, this theme will be strengthened and contrasted with the faster paced, much more violent and emotionally isolated world of the hero, a big-city cop.

By the end of this opening, we have a sense of the time, place and mood of the movie.

The Catalyst

Also referred to as the "inciting incident," this event really starts the story in motion. After we've been briefly introduced to the main characters, something significant happens. It can be as big as a murder or explosion, or as small as a kitten getting stuck in a tree. Whatever it is, from that point on, we know what the story is about and what the spine of the plot will be.

A catalyst can be an action or event, information conveyed through dialogue or a situation. In *Witness*, a murder occurs and the hero is called in to solve it.

The Central Question

This catalyst alone isn't enough, however. There is a central question at the heart of every movie. It is asked at the beginning of the movie, and it must be answered in the climax. In *Witness,* the question revolves around whether or not the hero will catch the killer. In *Schindler's List*, the question is "Will Schindler save 'his' Jews from the Nazis?" In any romantic comedy, the question is "Will boy get girl?"

In most movies, the answer to the question is "yes." If it's "no," then the movie is probably a tragedy.

Act One Development

Before we reach the first turning point that leads the story into Act Two, there is other information that must be in place. We need to know more about the main characters, the back story and the situation. What's the motivation of the protagonist? Who's the antagonist or antagonistic force? What's the central conflict between the main characters?

A beat is a single dramatic moment or event. Placed in order, several beats comprise a scene. Scenes comprise acts. And acts comprise your screenplay.

In *Witness* the following beats comprise the central action of Act One: trying to find the killer.

John Book shows Samuel, the Amish boy who witnessed the murder, a suspect. Samuel doesn't identify him.

John arranges for Rachel and Samuel to stay with his divorced sister and her children.

John shows Samuel a lineup of suspects.

John has Samuel look at books of mug shots.

Samuel inadvertently sees a photo of McFee, the corrupt cop who committed the murder, and points this out to John.

John tells his boss, Schaeffer.

McFee ambushes John, wounding him. John realizes that his boss and friend, Schaeffer, is corrupt, also.

At this point, everything we need to know to set the story in motion has been shown. We know what kind of movie we're watching, who the main characters are, what their conflict will be and what's at stake.

Turning Points

One of the most scathing criticisms that can be levelled at any screenplay is that it's too predictable and lacks surprises. A story holds our interest by virtue of its twists and turns. These unpredictable twists, turns and surprises can, and should, happen throughout your story.

But the really big surprises usually occur at two well-defined places in the script—at the end of Act One and end of Act Two. They literally turn the story in a new direction, often taking it to a new location or arena. There are new events and new decisions that must be made by the main characters. This accomplishes several things: It raises the central question again, and at the same time raises the stakes; it forces the protagonist to make more of a commitment to the goal; and it energetically moves the story into the next phase, or act.

Usually, the first turning point happens anywhere from fifteen to thirty minutes into a movie. The second occurs about twenty to thirty minutes before the end.

In *Witness*, the first turning point occurs about thirty minutes into the film, when the hero is ambushed by one of the henchmen of the villain. Since the only person he confided in was his boss, he knows this means the corruption reaches far higher than he realized. He doesn't know who to trust. He and the heroine and her son are all in grave danger. The central question is raised again: Will he get the killer? And the stakes are raised, because now he knows the killer is a cop.

The hero must save himself and the woman and her child. He does this by making a decision to get them out of the city and back to the security of their home.

There are actually two events that comprise the turning point from Act One to Act Two. The first is the ambush, which sends the hero, heroine and child back to Amish country. The second is the collapse of the hero, who is now reluctantly forced to remain in Amish country until he can heal. Thus, Act Two is going to take place in a different setting from the majority of the action of Act One. Most of what happens in Act Two will be a consequence of this change in location.

Second Turning Point

The second turning point does exactly what the first one did—it moves the story into a new direction, raises the central question again, raises the stakes, requires an even greater commitment on the part of the hero, and pushes the plot into the next, and final, act. But the second turning point also drastically speeds up the action, making the final act the most intense of all.

In *Witness*, the second turning point occurs when the villain discovers where the hero is hiding out and comes after him with his henchmen. This is set up via several quick beats:

John learns that his partner has been killed by the bad guys.

He tells the villain, Paul, that he's going to get him.

Several teenage thugs threaten the Amish, and John defends them, which is very un-Amish-like behavior. The local sheriff hears of this and realizes this man must be the one the city cops have been looking for. He tells Paul where John is staying.

All of that inevitably leads to the climactic action sequence: the final shoot-out between the hero and the villain.

Climax

The climax is pretty much the end of your story, so it should happen within a minute, or at most a few minutes, of the end of the movie. It's the ultimate confrontation between protagonist and antagonist, the moment when the problem is solved, the goal is reached, the central question is answered conclusively. Ideally, it should be a big finish—either literally big, in terms of action, or emotionally big, in terms of being moving.

In *Witness*, John defeats the bad guys, and there's nothing left but the final good-bye between John and Rachel.

Now there's nothing left to do but write "The End."

Problems With Structure

Several things can contribute to poor structure. If the setup is too slow, the audience will lose interest. This is one of the most common structural problems, and it can be deadly, because audiences have come to expect a fast pace. You have to hook them quickly. Some films take too long to get to the first turning point (a criticism of the otherwise charming movie, *Waking Ned Devine*). Some movies rush the second turning point, causing Act Three to seem to go on forever. And a few films have an extended resolution that goes on far too long. This last flaw can leave the audience feeling as if the filmmaker didn't know where to end the movie.

To avoid these problems, ask yourself the following questions when you've finished your screenplay:

- Does your first page have a strong visual image that conveys the mood and theme of the story?
- Is there a clear and strong catalyst, or inciting incident, early in the story?
- Does the central question inherently lead to the climax of your story? (For instance, in *Witness*, by asking, "Will John catch the killer?" we inevitably set in motion a plot that culminates in a climax where John confronts the killer.)
- Does each turning point raise the central question again?
- Are the turning points clear and dramatic?
- Is your climax exciting and satisfying?
- Is your resolution very brief?

The Sagging Middle

Many writers feel that Act Two, the longest act in a screenplay, is the most challenging. They struggle to keep it from becoming slow or boring. You must keep the momentum of the story, and at the same time not lose sight of your focus. Act Two is often where stories go offtrack, leaving the spine of the plot to wander off on a tangent.

The best way to prevent this is to make certain every scene in your script, especially in Act Two, occurs as a direct result of the preceding scene, moves the story forward and is absolutely necessary to either character or plot development. When scenes are connected in a clear and compelling cause-and-effect sequence, the momentum builds and the audience doesn't lose interest.

That doesn't mean that every scene deals only with the main characters or main plot. Some scenes must, of necessity, focus on subplots or supporting characters. But every scene must be composed of action-reaction. The end of Act One in *Witness* is a good example of cause and effect.

Samuel points to the photo of McFee as the killer.

This propels us into the next scene: John tells Schaeffer about McFee.

This leads to the next scene: John is ambushed by McFee and realizes that Schaeffer must be part of the corruption.

This results in John getting Rachel and Samuel out of the city, to the relative safety of Amish country.

Because of his wound, John becomes unconscious, and Rachel must care for him.

As you can see, there isn't an extraneous beat in this sequence of beats. Every action has a logical and dramatic reaction. This continually drives the story forward and doesn't allow the momentum to slow or come to a halt. Action-reaction scenes give your screenplay direction, focus and momentum.

Action Points

Events or developments that propel the story forward are called action points. The turning points are the main action points in a script, but there are others, as well. These other action points are particularly helpful in keeping Act Two fast-paced and entertaining. They are the barrier, the complication and the reversal.

A barrier is something that stops the protagonist dead in his tracks and forces him to choose an alternate plan or route. But don't stop your character for long, or the story will become boring. When confronted by a barrier, the character must quickly devise a way around it.

In *Witness*, the villain tries to find out where the hero is hiding out. He asks the local sheriff to call around to the various Amish farms, but is told that's impossible—the Amish don't have telephones. He then interrogates the hero's partner, who refuses to talk. Another barrier.

It's important to remember not to repeat the same type of barrier, otherwise it becomes redundant and loses its dramatic impact.

A complication is an event or development that the audience knows is going to have repercussions down the line. Anticipating the inevitable reaction to the complication is a big part of the fun. For instance, in *Working Girl*, Melanie Griffith plays a secretary who pretends to be an executive to get past the typing pool prejudice that is keeping her from advancing in her company. The audience anticipates that at some point both her boss and the fellow executive she's falling in love with, will learn the awful truth: She's *just* a secretary.

67

The final action point is a reversal. It totally turns the story around and can involve a physical change in direction, or an emotional one. Romantic stories, especially romantic comedies, often rely on the standard reversal of two characters who dislike each other, then discover they're falling in love.

These action points can all be used to keep up the momentum of your story.

Subplots

Every movie has at least one, usually more, subplots. A commonly held view is that the plot carries the action of a movie, while the subplot carries the theme. For instance, in *Witness* the plot is about crooked cops stealing confiscated drugs in order to sell them. Most of the action that takes place in the film revolves around this plot. The subplot is the romantic relationship between the hero and heroine. This relationship expresses the theme of the movie: the need for connection through community.

The subplot is often what the movie is "really" about. It's where the writer's passion lies. It was necessary to have a strong, action-oriented plot in *Witness*. But what I really cared about was the subplot, and the exploration of how two very different people, from opposite worlds, overcome the gulf between them and fall in love.

A subplot dimensionalizes a screenplay, making it much more than just the linear progression of the plot. Often, a subplot provides an opportunity to have the kind of character development that the plot doesn't have time for. Without the romantic subplot of *Witness*, the hero was just another tough cop. With it, he was vulnerable and sensitive, and experienced tremendous growth and change. He became a memorable character, as opposed to a forgettable, stereotypical one.

The subplot of *Witness* elevated the movie above a conventional cop movie like so many that get made every year. It is also rather unique in that the subplot takes over for most of Act Two. The plot, centering on the question of whether or not the hero will catch the killer, is the focus of Act One and provides momentum and jeopardy in the movie. But the subplot, centering on the romantic relationship, becomes the focus of Act Two. Then in Act Three we return to the plot, with the final confrontation between the hero and the villain.

The John-Rachel subplot has a clear beginning, middle and end. The setup takes place in Act One when they meet. The central question is soon established: Will John and Rachel get together, despite their profound differences? The first turning point happens at the beginning of Act Two, when Rachel nurses the wounded John back to health. During this time, the initial conflict between them turns to attraction, then love. Their relationship grows during Act Two, especially during a scene where they dance in a barn. The second turning point occurs when they acknowledge their feelings for each other by kissing passionately, thus raising the stakes of their relationship and repeating the central question: Will they get together?

In the *Witness* romantic subplot, the turning points occur immediately after the turning points in the main plot.

The plot is often referred to as the "A" story and the subplots as the "B," "C," etc. stories.

The plot line (A) and the subplot line (B) of *Witness* dovetail this way:

Setup
(A) The murder   (B) John/Rachel meet

First Turning Point
(A) Ambush of John   (B) Rachel nurses John

Second Turning Point
(A) John hits teenage thug   (B) John/Rachel kiss

Climax
(A) Villain is defeated   (B) John saves Rachel

Resolution
(A) John reconnects with police   (B) John/Rachel say good-bye

Generally speaking, it isn't a good idea to have the subplot take over as it does in *Witness*. But even in that film, the plot momentum was kept going by repeatedly returning to the plot situation. The hero telephoned his partner, who told him of developments in the murder case; the partner was interrogated, then killed by the bad cops; and the hero was forced to respond to the death of his partner by calling the villain.

Subplots are structured just as plots are—in three acts, with a beginning, middle and end. And they must be an integral part of the overall story. You can't just throw in a subplot because it sounds interesting. It must directly relate to the main plot.

Ask yourself the following questions.

- Is this subplot necessary? Does it dovetail naturally with the plot and add to it?
- Do I have too many subplots? (Usually more than two or three is a problem.)
- Does each subplot have a clear three-act structure, with strong turning points?
- Is my subplot resolved at about the same place in the screenplay that the plot is resolved?" (The climax of the subplot should be near the climax of the plot.)

The best way to learn structure is to rent movies in the genre you want to write in. Outline them as you watch them, then compare each outline to learn the "rules" of structure followed in that genre.

9 Conflict

One of the most common reasons screenplays are rejected is because the conflict simply isn't compelling enough. Conflict can determine the strength, or weakness, of your script. When an executive or producer tells a writer, "Your script needs more punch," or "It's flat," what she's really saying is it lacks conflict.

Drama is conflict. This is true no matter what genre you're writing in—action, comedy, romance or sci-fi. Conflict stems from two characters having mutually exclusive goals. Only one can win. The plot is all about the protagonist and antagonist fighting each other to achieve their goals.

Conflicts come in all sizes, shapes and degrees. They can be overt—fights, car chases, shouting matches, etc.—or subtle—an unhappily married couple sitting silently over dinner at a restaurant.

There are five types of conflict:

1. Interior conflict that takes place within a character. For instance, when Hamlet agonizes over "to be or not to be," he is contemplating suicide.
2. Conflict in relationships.
3. Situational conflict arising out of a particular place and time.
4. General societal conflict; for example, between social classes or ethnic groups.
5. Spiritual; for instance, between a person and God or the devil.

Interior Conflict

When a character is deeply torn about how to feel or what to do, this is interior conflict. The challenge, of course, is how to show this conflict onscreen. An inexperienced writer might resort to a voice-over narration. This does work in rare circumstances. An exceptional example is the brilliant 1970s movie, *Days of Heaven*. When the movie was first screened, it wasn't well received. Somehow, it fell flat. So the director (Terrence Malick of *The*

Thin Red Line) went back and had the young sister of the protagonist do a voice-over, giving her feelings about what was happening. Because this character's voice was fresh and unique and emotionally compelling, the voice-over worked.

But in most cases, using a voice-over is a cop-out for a writer. The best way to reveal a character's inner conflict is to do so through his actions or dialogue.

Following is a scene from the African-American female ensemble drama *Waiting to Exhale*, written by Terry McMillan and Ron Bass, and based on her best-selling novel. Gloria (Loretta Devine), a single mother, has had a serious disagreement with her would-be boyfriend, Marvin (Gregory Hines). He encouraged her son, who she dotes on, to go away to school, and she was furious with him. Now she comes to apologize:

EXT. MARVIN'S HOUSE—EVENING

Gloria looks nervous as she knocks on Marvin's front door. It's RAINING again but she doesn't seem to mind.

                    MARVIN
                (o.s.)
          It's open.

She enters. He's refinishing an old chair in the middle of the room. Gloria's admiring it. And him. From outside, we hear THUNDER.

                    GLORIA
          How you been doing? Haven't seen much of you lately.

He's sanding away. Doesn't look up at her.

                    MARVIN
          Been a little busy.

She wants to sit down, but he's not acting like he wants her to . . .

                    GLORIA
          I think I know why.

> (beat)
> I acted silly, when all you did was tell me the truth.
> (beat)
> I guess I didn't want to hear it.

Marvin doesn't look up. Keeps working. Gloria takes a deep breath. This is hard for her.

> GLORIA
> I came over for two reasons. I know I shut you out. And I miss you in my life. Our life.
> (breath)
> There's no doubt in my mind that you were right. And I apologize.

Now Marvin finally looks up. Stops sanding. He nods toward the sofa.

> MARVIN
> (softly)
> Come on and sit down.

She does. Slowly. Purple lightning illuminates the sky outside. Rain beats against the window behind her.

> GLORIA
> I didn't want him to leave. I've invested all my hopes and dreams in that boy. But this is about more than just missing him. It's about the *way* I was fixing to miss him.

One of the hardest things she's ever had to say.

> GLORIA
> *He's* been the man in my life. My companion. More than just my child, you know . . .

Marvin already knows this. But his eyes are so intent. She looks down. Somehow, her breath is coming faster now. CLOSE on her . . .

73

> GLORIA
> ...I gave up the dream of having someone for myself a long time ago. It was a terrible thing for me to do to Tarik...

When she looks up, he is sitting next to her. A quiet storm.

> GLORIA
> ...I'm grateful to you. For opening my eyes.

He's not smiling. Why isn't he smiling? What's he thinking? Her breath even faster. Jesus.

> GLORIA
> ...for not allowing my fears of being lonely to deny Tarik a chance to grow up and do what he wants to. I was so unfair.

Marvin is putting his arm around her shoulder, comforting her...

> MARVIN
> You were being unfair to you. Do you understand? You've made yourself believe that you're not worthy of somebody wanting to love you...

Gloria is embarrassed and her eyes are getting cloudy because this is the truth she's denied for so long. And now here's this man telling her.

> MARVIN
> ...I won't let you do that anymore.

And now she's crying and Marvin bends over and kisses her tears.

In this beautifully written, intensely emotional and touching scene, we see different levels of conflict: between Marvin and Gloria, and within Gloria herself. This conflict is revealed through dialogue and action.

Another way to express inner conflict is to have the character do something physical; for instance, an out-of-control parent who's very angry at his child, but doesn't want to hurt the child, might instead pick up the child's toy and smash it against a wall.

Conflict in Relationships

The strongest conflict in most movies centers on the mutually exclusive goals of the protagonist and antagonist. In romantic relationships, the conflict is equally as important as the attraction. Being clear about the nature of the conflict in every scene you write will keep your screenplay dramatic and focused.

Societal Conflict

This is often expressed as conflict between a person and a group whose actions or beliefs he opposes. It can also be expressed as conflict between two or more groups. Some of the strongest movies have been about a lone person pitted against a powerful system (*To Kill a Mockingbird, The Killing Fields*). When the theme of a movie has to do with prejudice or injustice, the conflict is often societal. In this kind of story, the antagonist, or antagonistic force, usually represents wrong, and the lone, courageous hero represents right.

Situational Conflict

Perhaps the ultimate example of conflict engendered by a situation is *Titanic*. The ship is sinking. There aren't enough lifeboats. Only a few people can be saved. That's pretty dramatic stuff. But if that were all that was involved, it wouldn't be enough to make this the most commercially successful movie of all time. What lifted it to that dizzy height was the personal conflict brought out by this situational conflict.

The hero and heroine, Jack and Rose, were in conflict because she had the chance to get in a lifeboat but didn't want to leave him. Jack was in conflict with Rose's evil fiancé, who wanted him to die.

Adding to this was conflict among the supporting characters, who reacted to the life-or-death situation in different ways. Some were brave, others cowardly. Husbands and wives had to make agonizing decisions about separating or dying together. Parents tried desperately to save their children. And there was a powerful class conflict shown by the fact that the first-class passengers were put in lifeboats first, while those in steerage were locked below deck.

If the situational conflict of the sinking ship hadn't been personalized through the characters and their relationships, the movie would have been merely an impressive special-effects achievement that didn't touch our hearts and make us want to see it over and over again.

Spiritual Conflict

It is rare, but often very successful, to have a movie focus on conflict between a character and God or the devil. In *Amadeus*, Salieri hates Mozart but his real conflict is with God, who created his brilliant competitor. *The Prince of Egypt* is about Moses' developing relationship with God. And *Ghost* is about the hero, Patrick Swayze, coming to terms with the fact that he has died and needs to move on (to heaven). In *Rosemary's Baby*, the heroine, Mia Farrow, is up against the devil himself, who has fathered her child.

But in these stories, we don't see God or the devil as a character in the film. The protagonist's problems with the invisible spiritual force are projected onto a character who's in his way.

Problems and Solutions

The single biggest problem with conflict is that it simply isn't strong enough. It's one thing to have a conservative Democrat or Republican arguing with a liberal Democrat or Republican. Their disagreement may be interesting, but probably not all that powerful. However, if you have a white, upper-class, male conservative Republican from the religious right arguing with a black, lower-class, female liberal Democrat from a politically active ghetto church . . . get the picture? Their conflict, which is cultural, socioeconomic, religious and gender-based, would certainly be strong—and very exciting to watch onscreen.

It's critical that the conflict be expressed in a clear line throughout the screenplay. The goals of the protagonist and antagonist must be seen to be diametrically opposed. Conflict must be expressed in the strongest possible visual and emotional terms. It isn't enough for your hero to say to the villain, "I'll do my best to see to it that you're defeated." Instead, he must vow to stop him, no matter what the cost.

Conflict between the main characters and supporting characters is also important. In *You've Got Mail* there's a running conflict between the Tom

Hanks character, who gradually realizes he wants an old-fashioned romantic relationship, and his father, who's gone through multiple marriages, never truly caring for any of his wives.

Take a hard look at the conflict in your story. Is it truly compelling enough? If so, you're well on your way to having a story that works.

 Scenes

"Scene" is defined by screenwriting guru Robert McKee as "an action through conflict in more or less continuous time and space that turns the value-charged condition of a character's life on at least one value with a degree of perceptible significance." In plain language, a scene is about a single event or development that impacts the characters or plot, turning a negative situation positive, or vice versa. Whatever "value" is at stake in the character's life, or in the plot, at the beginning of the scene—safety, love, hate, jeopardy—must be changed by the end of the scene.

If what's at stake in the scene is the same at the end as it was at the beginning, the scene doesn't move the story forward. And if a scene doesn't impact either the characters or the plot in a meaningful way necessary to move the story forward, it is redundant.

But, you may say, you need a particular scene for "exposition." If that's the only reason it's there, and it doesn't change the characters or the plot, then it will be flat and uninteresting. You need to find another more entertaining way to get across that exposition.

For instance, say you have a character who's overweight and trying desperately to stay on a diet. You could have a scene where she discusses with a friend how difficult it is to pass up the calorie-rich foods she loves in favor of low-fat dishes. This would be downright boring and wouldn't move the plot forward or deepen the character in any way. The situation, and the character, are the same at the end of the scene as they are at the beginning.

Instead, show don't tell. Have a scene where the character is staring hungrily at a rich dessert. She knows she shouldn't have it, but boy does it look delicious. Finally, she can't stand it. She takes a bite, then another, and we can see that she's going to binge. Suddenly, she sees the photo of a thin model that she taped to her refrigerator door to inspire herself to stick to the diet. She hesitates, looks at the photo, then at the dessert, then back at the photo. An expression of determination comes over her face. Grabbing the dessert, she takes it outside to the trash can and throws it inside, slamming the lid firmly on the can. As she goes back inside, she's smiling proudly.

See how the "value" changed from the beginning of the scene to the end? At the beginning she wavered in her goal, but by the end she made real progress in achieving it.

Every scene in your screenplay should "turn" in this way.

In addition to a change in value, how do you decide if a scene is necessary?

Unnecessary Scenes

William Goldman tells the following apocryphal story behind the writing of *Butch Cassidy and the Sundance Kid*. In researching these outlaws, Goldman read that the immensely likable Butch found himself in jail at one point. Butch assured the governor that if he would pardon him, Butch would leave the state and never rob banks or trains in that state again. He would do it elsewhere. The governor pardoned him, and Butch kept his word.

Goldman loved this scene. It was the primary inspiration for telling the story of Butch and Sundance. But when he wrote the script, he couldn't make that scene fit naturally into it; there was no place for it. Finally, Goldman reluctantly threw it out. The true-life event that inspired the movie isn't in it.

No matter how enamored you may be of a particular scene, no matter how wonderful it may be on its own, if it isn't necessary and integral to the story, it doesn't belong.

Blocking a Scene

Every scene must have a beginning, middle and end, just as your screenplay does. It must have a main character with a goal, an opponent with an opposite goal, and an escalating battle between them, preferably ending with some degree of self-revelation on the part of the main character. This "battle" doesn't have to be particularly big, and it doesn't have to be physical.

For example, in the famous scene in *Five Easy Pieces* where Jack Nicholson's character is trying to order toast, the battle with the recalcitrant waitress is purely a war of words. She insists they don't offer wheat toast on the menu, and there are no substitutions. He asks her to make a chicken sandwich, which they do have on the menu, and put it on wheat toast. When she says OK, he tells her to leave off the chicken. That way, he'll get his wheat toast. At this point, the waitress throws up her hands in anger, and Nicholson ends up leaving the restaurant without being served.

Academy Award-winning screenwriter Ron Bass (*Rain Man*) describes how he blocks a scene, or "prewrites" it, before actually writing it: "I figure it out before I ever start to write the script: What are all the things that are going to go into this scene? What's everybody gonna feel? Where's the start? Where does it end? What's the informational content? The emotional content? The dramatic tone? What are the character changes? What's everybody thinking and feeling? What's the setting gonna look like?"

In blocking a scene you must ask yourself the following questions. Do this with every single scene in your screenplay.

- Understand the purpose of the scene. What is your objective? It must contribute to the hero's inner or outer motivation in some way. How do you make this story's point?
- What is the conflict, especially the emotional conflict, between the characters in the scene?
- What is each character's objective? What do they want and why do they want it? Desire gives the scene and the story drive, and determines action and dialogue.
- What is each character's attitude? How do they feel about what's going on?
- What is the most entertaining and effective way to get across the information in this scene—physical action, visual sensibility or dialogue? (Dialogue should always be the last choice.)
- Have I given this scene only as much length as is absolutely necessary? The rhythm of a film is set by the length of scenes. If they're too long, the film will be deadly dull and slow (*Meet Joe Black*). The average scene is anywhere from one and one-half to three minutes long. Rarely are scenes longer than that.
- Could I combine this scene with another to increase the pace and still make the story point I need to make?
- Does this scene relate to the protagonist's plan, either directly or indirectly?

Each scene should end with the individual issue that is at the heart of it resolved, but with something more important left unresolved, compelling the viewer to continue watching the movie. The scene should end on a higher note of drama or comedy than it began on. As a highly successful TV movie director says, "End the scene on the highest point of drama, preferably on a question that isn't answered until the next scene. That way you go into the next scene in motion, and there is an emotional continuity from scene to scene."

Components of Scene Design

The four primary components of scene design are turning points, setups/payoffs, emotional dynamics and choice.

Because a scene is a story in miniature, it must have what a larger story has: turning points. The main character in a scene (who may be the protagonist or a supporting character) has to make a choice or a decision, take an action or react to something that has happened. When he acts, there is a result he didn't anticipate. This turns the scene in a different direction. Turning points must involve surprise, raise the viewer's level of curiosity, reveal insight into the plot or character, and point the story in a new direction.

With setups and payoffs, you layer in information about something, then later in the screenplay you "pay it off" by using this information in a significant way.

Emotional transitions are perhaps the most critical aspect of a scene. An audience experiences emotion by empathizing with the characters. To do this we must understand what the characters want, and we must care about whether or not they get it. It's critical not to try to elicit the same emotion in the audience over and over again, without variation. If you write a tremendously sad scene, an audience will be touched. If it's followed by another sad scene, the audience will be slightly less (not more) touched, because they're beginning to anesthetize themselves to it. And if you pile on even more sad scenes, the audience will actively pull away, because they can only take so much. Scenes must vary in emotional intensity. When you've put an audience through a particularly tough scene, follow it with a lighter one to give the audience some breathing room.

Some of the most successful films take advantage of the "laughter through tears" emotional arc. If you can make an audience cry, then get them to laugh, or vice versa, you've hit on a full range of emotions.

Choice is the final element of scene design. To be dramatic or humorous it must involve a true dilemma—not between good and bad, but between

81

irreconcilable goods or the lesser of two evils. From the character's point of view, two things are desirable, but he can only choose one. Or two things are bad (*Sophie's Choice* is a powerful example), but he must choose one. Which will it be? The decision is tough—a true dilemma.

Sequence

Sometimes a series of scenes—usually anywhere from two to five, occasionally more—are grouped together in a sequence. They're tied together by a central ministory line, with its own beginning, middle and end. A situation is set up in the beginning, it builds in the middle, then reaches a climax at the end, without any interruption from subplots.

Most scene sequences are short, just a few minutes. *The Apostle* opens with the following compelling sequence.

- The protagonist, a Pentecostal minister played by Robert Duvall, is driving down a rural road with his mother.
- He sees that a terrible multicar accident has occurred and victims are still inside the cars.
- Stopping, he goes to a dying passenger in a car and prays for him.
- A state trooper tells the minister he can't be there, he's in the way. The minister insists he's saving a soul.
- The minister gets back in his car and drives off, convinced that he just did some good.

In this brief sequence, we learn so much—who the movie will be about (the minister), what kind of character he is (a man of true faith) and the setting (the rural South). All of this is tied together by a single unifying event: a car accident.

 Dialogue

Writing good dialogue is one of the greatest challenges most writers face. It must sound as if it's the way people really talk—only briefer, more clever and to the point.

Before knuckling down to the challenge of writing scintillating dialogue that will effortlessly flow out of the mouths of actors, you must first understand exactly what you're trying to accomplish in that particular scene. To repeat what we discussed in the previous chapter, ask yourself the following questions.

- What is my objective within this scene?
- How is the scene going to end?
- What is each character's objective within the scene?
- What is each character's attitude?
- How will the scene begin?

Only when you know the answers to those questions can you focus on the dialogue you need to write in a scene. Ideally, dialogue should come last, after you have decided where your story is going. By deciding what the point of the scene is and cutting out everything extraneous to this, you will have sharp, focused dialogue.

The truth about dialogue is that less is more. Film is a visual medium. It's much better to show than to tell. Never use dialogue when action will work just as well. Remember that the first movies were silent, and they worked quite successfully.

How do you determine when to use dialogue? When it is necessary to accomplish one or more of the following three things:

1. Give information.
2. Move your story forward.
3. Reveal insights into character.

If your dialogue doesn't do one of those things, it isn't necessary. Never write dialogue that is merely small talk. In real life, people do a lot of this. ("Hi, how are you?" "Just fine. And you?" "Not bad.") This sort of thing slows down a script and is downright boring. All dialogue must be essential and have a purpose.

Another thing that will slow down your screenplay (and irritate actors enormously) is to use a lot of parenthetical directions—telling the actors how to read the lines. While it is sometimes necessary, it should be done sparingly.

The shorter your dialogue, the better. Use short speeches and crisp dialogue. Interruptions and pauses make dialogue sound natural, the way people really talk, since most of us don't usually speak in complete, grammatically perfect sentences.

Don't be afraid to choose silence over words. Silence can be golden, more impactive and emotional than flowery phrases. At the end of *Witness*, when the hero and heroine see each other for the last time, neither speaks; they simply look at each other. The emotion each is feeling comes through in their facial expressions and body language.

There are three major mistakes made in writing dialogue. The biggest and most common mistake most writers, especially inexperienced ones, make is in having every character sound alike. There's little, if any, differentiation in their style of speech—vocabulary, rhythm, etc. A poorly educated blue-collar worker sounds just like a well-educated judge. A female character sounds like a male. And a teenager sounds like a senior citizen.

Before you write dialogue, try to get inside your character. Be still and silent and focused, and listen for your character's voice. Ask yourself what that kind of character would sound like. Keep in mind the time and place he has come from. An independent, liberated woman of the 1990s would sound different than a dependent, repressed housewife of the 1950s. Dialogue must be appropriate for that particular character.

The test that is often applied to dialogue to determine if it is character-specific is this: Cover up the character's name and just read the dialogue. Can you tell from the dialogue which character is speaking? You should be able to do so.

The second common mistake made by novice writers is writing "on the nose." This means writing dialogue that is obvious. Answering a direct question with a direct answer is a perfect example of on-the-nose dialogue. For instance, one character asks another, "How are you?" The other character answers, "I'm not feeling well. I'm afraid I may have a serious illness."

A better way to do this would be to have the second character not respond directly to the question. He might change the subject, thereby suggesting that he doesn't want to talk about how he's feeling because he's worried that something may be very wrong.

One of the most frequent instances of on-the-nose dialogue happens when one character says, "I love you," to another character, who replies, "I love you, too." Carrie Fisher, who segued from an acting career (*Star Wars*) to a highly successful writing career, says that she never has a character say, "I love you." She finds other, more indirect ways to express that feeling.

A perfect example is the end of *When Harry Met Sally*. When the Billy Crystal character tells the Meg Ryan character he has just realized he wants to spend the rest of his life with her, she responds, "I hate you, Harry. I really, really hate you." But the way she's looking at him, and her tone of voice, are saying just the opposite—she loves him.

The third common mistake made in writing dialogue is writing long speeches. When writing dialogue, remember less is more. Most dialogue is only two or three lines long. If you read a well-written screenplay, you'll see that the dialogue is almost like watching a tennis match. A character says something brief, the other character responds, and it goes back and forth, like a tennis ball being quickly batted back and forth. It's a constant exchange of power that can be sexual, physical, political or social.

One way to learn how to write good dialogue is to listen to the people around you. Overhear conversations in public places. Pay attention to how your friends and family speak. Listen to the tone and cadence of their speech. Notice that each person has his own particular speech pattern and phrases that he likes to use repeatedly. A character who uses a word like "golly" is going to be very different than a character who uses profanity.

Dialogue must be dramatic. It should create emotional conflict between characters, which will build tension. If you always have conflict and tension, you won't lose the audience's interest.

When Actors Write Dialogue

Nowadays many actors are also writers. Because they know so much about how to speak dialogue, they tend to be especially good at writing it. Some advice from actor/writers:

Stanley Tucci (*Big Night*): "I was encountering a lot of scripts where the dialogue seemed imposed upon the characters. [It] didn't come from the characters—it was the writer stuffing these words into their mouths and they were forced to spit them back out again. Trying to act them was tortuous."

Carrie Fisher (*Postcards From the Edge*): "Writing, you envision what would be easiest for you to say because you've been there." She goes on to say, "In real life, people don't talk straight out in sentences, but in very particular ways."

Billy Bob Thornton (*Sling Blade*): "Sometimes words look really good on paper. They're flowery, intense and just look great and when you read them, it's like, 'Wow, that's beautiful.' But then as an actor, you try to say those words, and they don't sound right. So when I write, I don't try to make it look good on paper. I write for it to sound good when it's said."

Believable dialogue creates believable characters. Actors need to understand their characters' motivations, no matter how small the role. That knowledge should come out in the writing.

Keys to Good Dialogue
- It's like a piece of music. It has a rhythm of its own.
- It's short and spare.
- It conveys conflict, attitudes, intentions. Instead of telling about a character, it *reveals* character through speech patterns, vocabulary, accent and length of sentences.
- It's easily spoken by an actor because of its natural rhythm.
- It reveals a character's cultural or ethnic background, education, age, etc.
- It reveals a character's values.

Signs of Bad Dialogue
- It's wooden, stilted, awkward and hard to speak.
- All characters sound alike, without reference to their differing backgrounds.
- It's too direct—"on the nose." Rather than suggesting or hinting, it spells out every thought and feeling a character has.
- It tells everything, rather than allowing things to be revealed through subtext.

One of the best ways to tell if your dialogue is good or bad is to read it out loud. Hear it as you're saying it. Perhaps even record it, then listen to it. It can be enormously helpful to have amateur or professional actors do a "reading" of your script. When you hear other people speak your dialogue, it will be painfully obvious what is wrong with it.

Exposition

Exposition is information necessary to convey to the audience so they can fully understand the story and characters. The challenge lies in conveying that information in a way that doesn't bore the socks off the audience. Often, the best or only way to get across certain exposition is through dialogue. How do you write this kind of expository dialogue so it isn't dull? Through conflict and dramatic action, so the audience isn't aware that they're being spoon-fed hard information. Have your characters discuss critical information while doing something exciting. (A lovemaking scene can be a perfect opportunity for a character to reveal necessary information.) Put emotional intensity into the information by giving it during a time of crisis.

The worst thing you can do is have expository dialogue sound like a dry, dull lecture. Make it dramatic and fun and interesting.

Speeches

There are times in your screenplay when you will need to let a character deliver a longer speech. This should only be done when absolutely necessary and should address an especially significant issue in your story. Here's how this speech should be structured:
- The beginning should state the premise of the speech.
- The middle of the speech should intensify the character's feeling or attitude.
- The end, or finish, is the "punch" position, the convincer. Ideally, the speech should build to an effective closing phrase.

You'll notice when you watch a scene in a movie, that often (and certainly in the most important scenes) a character will end the scene with a particularly telling piece of dialogue. This "rounds out" or "finishes off" the scene, just as a nice dessert finishes off a meal. It completes it. It also, hopefully, piques the audience's interest regarding the next scene.

The following scene from *Jerry Maguire* exemplifies many of these dialogue issues. Jerry, played by Tom Cruise, is a sports agent who has gone from the pinnacle of success to fighting desperately to hang onto one (very difficult) client, Rod Tidwell, played by Cuba Gooding Jr. Jerry is deeply attracted to his assistant, Dorothy, a single mom, but doesn't want to make a commitment to her. He asks Rod, a happily married man, for advice:

> JERRY
> What do you know about dating a single mother?

Tidwell warms to the personal question.

> TIDWELL
> Oh, I know plenty. I was raised by a single mother.

> JERRY
> Tell me, because it's been a month, and she's about to take another job in San Diego.

Tidwell is always happy to hold forth.

> TIDWELL
> First, single mothers don't "date." They have *been to the circus*, you know what I'm saying? They have been to the puppet show and they have *seen the strings*. You love her?

> JERRY
> How do I know?

> TIDWELL
> You know when you know. It makes you shivver, it eats at your insides. You know?

> JERRY
> No, I don't know.

> TIDWELL
> Then you gotta have The Talk.

JERRY
But I sure don't like that she's leaving.

TIDWELL
Well, that ain't fair to her. A single mother, that's a sacred thing, man.

JERRY
The kid is amazing.

TIDWELL
No. A real man does not shoplift the "pooty" from a single mom.

JERRY
I didn't "shoplift the pooty." We were thrown together and—I mean it's two mutual people who—
            (a look)
Alright, I shoplifted the pooty.

TIDWELL
Shame on you. SHAME on you.

Notice how brief each character's dialogue is—usually just two or three lines. It goes back and forth, in a quick exchange, rather than one character speaking at length while the other listens.

Compare the different speech patterns. Tidwell's is more "street smart" and blunt, reflecting his poor, inner-city roots and in-your-face personality. Jerry's is more educated and less straightforward, because agents can rarely afford to be honest and direct. If you covered up the names, you could still tell who was speaking.

The exchange is clever and fun, and there is clear conflict, both internally and externally. Jerry is at war with himself, and to a lesser extent with Tidwell, and the dialogue reflects that.

Most important of all, this dialogue reveals a great deal about the characters without being "on the nose."

# 12 Subtext

All good screenplays have subtext, which is what the characters are *really* saying between the lines—the unspoken feelings that hide beneath the spoken words. It is that which is left unsaid. Usually characters are conscious of this, but often they're not. Instead of being direct and saying exactly what they mean, they say something that is intended to cover up their true feelings or attitudes. But even though these underlying drives and meanings may or may not be clear to the character, they must be clear to the audience.

One of the most overt and funny examples of subtext is in the Woody Allen film, *Annie Hall*. When the hero and heroine first meet, they look each other over carefully. They talk about photography in a very pseudo-intellectual way, trying to impress each other. But their subtext is written in subtitles onscreen, revealing what they're each really thinking. She worries that she may not be smart enough to appeal to him. He wonders if he's being shallow.

You can look at your own life to see how big a role subtext plays in it. How often do you feel like telling an annoying boss or co-worker to "go to hell"? But you don't because you need the job and the goodwill of the people you work with. Instead, you might pound a little harder on your computer keyboard, slam papers around or make a sarcastic comment that sounds like a joke but is actually serious. When you do that, you're using subtext.

Characters in screenplays behave the same way. They usually behave not as they really are, but how they want to appear. They do this for self-protection, self-esteem and to protect their ego. The key is to get the character to reveal himself, despite his efforts not to, through subtext.

In *City of Angels*, with Meg Ryan and Nicolas Cage, a man is about to undergo emergency heart surgery. As the anesthetic is beginning to take effect, the surgeon speaks to him:

SURGEON
Mr. Balford, it's Dr. Rice.

BALFORD
(groggy)
Hey. Hey, Dr. Rice. Will I be able to do stuff?

RICE
What do you want to do?

BALFORD
We have tickets to Paris. I want to jog down the Champs-Elysées.

Instead of having the patient ask, "Am I going to live or die?" the writer is much less "on the nose." The surgeon, and the audience, knows that's what he really means when he asks if he'll be able to "do stuff."

Subtext isn't just shown through dialogue. It is also shown through a character's actions. This can be literally having a character say one thing but do another. At the end of *Out of Sight*, based on the Elmore Leonard novel, the heroine, a cop, has captured the hero, a bank robber, who she's fallen in love with while chasing. She *says* she's taking him to prison, where she expects him to remain for many years. But she's arranged for him to be transported in a van with a fellow prisoner who's an expert at breaking out of prisons.

From Book to Screen: Adaptations

13

Hollywood has long had a love affair with books. Classics, popular fiction, serious nonfiction and even short stories all have been the center of book-to-film deals. Some recent examples of successful book-to-film projects include *I Know What You Did Last Summer*, *L.A. Confidential* and *Contact*. As both a screenwriter and a novelist, I've experienced all aspects of the book-to-film arena. I've adapted my own books to film, watched other people adapt my books and adapted other authors' books.

Many book authors are interested in adapting their stories to film. And many screenwriters find books a terrific source of material. The questions most often asked about the process of turning books into movies are:

- How do you successfully turn a book into a film, when the book is usually much longer than the movie can be?
- How do networks and studios choose which books to buy for film?
- Why do some books make good movies, while others don't?

While there are some exceptions, most notably in the independent film arena, most of the books optioned for film have a strong protagonist that a star will want to play. Movies are usually star-driven. Most movies get made because a star wants to act in it. *The Horse Whisperer* was a partial manuscript by a first-time novelist when it became the subject of an intense, six-figure bidding war. Robert Redford was willing to pay more than anyone else for the film rights, because he was determined to play the hero of that story. That character was enormously compelling and attractive—a star part. If the protagonist of the novel had been much less charismatic, the book wouldn't have become a film.

So what happens to a book like *The Prince of Tides* when a star like Barbra Streisand decides to direct and star in it? It's a big book, several hundred pages long, with multiple story lines and numerous significant characters. A screenplay is only about 120 pages (one page equals one minute of film, and most movies are no longer than two hours). Obviously, the story must be condensed to work as a movie. Which story does Ms. Streisand choose to focus on? The one that has a character *she* can play—a character who wasn't even one of the most important in the novel.

In addition to a highly castable protagonist, another requirement for a book-to-film deal is enough plot to drive a story. Many novels focus on the interior lives of the characters or the subtleties of relationships. There simply isn't enough happening to fill a two-hour movie. Movies are about what characters are doing, not what they're thinking. "Show, don't tell," is a screenwriting mantra. You must show what a character is thinking or feeling through his actions. But in novels, there can be a great deal of "telling" in the form of delving into the character's feelings and thoughts. When you read, you exercise your imagination. But film is a visual medium. You only see what's in front of the camera. You can't read the actor's minds.

How do you choose a book to adapt to film? First, it has to be attainable, in a legal sense.

Of Rights and Wrongs

The first step in acquiring the rights to a book, short story, play or true-life story is to ask yourself if this particular story is one you feel strongly enough about to make a commitment to writing the screenplay. The most satisfying story to tell is one that touches you personally and is, therefore, important to you. It should speak to your heart as a writer.

Eric Roth, whose script for *Forrest Gump* (based on the book by Winston Groom) brought him an Academy Award, said, "If you don't have a passion for, or a relationship with the material, you just won't find a voice with it."

Carl Franklin, the writer-director who brought Walter Mosley's *Devil in a Blue Dress* to the screen, adds: "If you read something that affects you, you start seeing scenes from it in your head. If you can't get those scenes out of your head, if you've been seduced by the source, you're not going to rest until you've taken it all the way to the screen."

The next step is finding out if those rights are available. A property can be in the public domain, meaning anyone can use it for any purpose. In the United States, a property registered for copyright after 1978 moves to the public domain fifty years after the author's death. Works registered before 1978 originally were copyrighted for twenty-eight years. But current law

93

makes it possible to renew a copyright for an additional forty-seven years, for a total coverage of seventy-five years.

If a work is not in public domain, you must contact the owner of the rights to it (usually the author or his estate) and ask about its availability. The book's publisher can give you the name of the person (usually an agent or lawyer) representing the rights-holder. If the rights-holder is willing, you can negotiate an option, which means giving you the exclusive right to adapt the book, and/or try to set it up at a studio, network, production company, etc.

Options come in all forms—no-cash, little cash or a great deal of cash— and they can last from as little as twenty-four hours to as long as several years. It's a good idea to have an agent or an entertainment attorney help you negotiate an option.

In the case of true-life stories, or real events, the rights to a story rest with the people who experienced it. These people can sell their life rights. Again, the options on life rights can be as flexible as the options on books, plays, short stories or magazine articles.

In both cases, the seller, the market and your financial resources will determine the details of the option.

To search the Library of Congress records for the owner of a particular copyright or to learn if a work is copyrighted, call (202) 707-6850. For general information on copyrights, contact the U.S. Copyright Office at (202) 707-3000, or their Internet site at http://lcweb.loc.gov/copyright.

The Art of Adaptation

Let's say you've optioned such a book or written a novel with enough action in its plot and with a protagonist who's interesting enough to appeal to a star. How do you adapt it? In adapting a book to film, the screenwriter has to find a way to tell the story, to lend cinematic shape to the material. Film is a different medium than books, not just in terms of length but in terms of different demands. In fiction you can write in a nonlinear structure, flashing back and forth in time, jumping from location to location, and going in and out of various characters' viewpoints. In film you must move the story forward at all times. And generally speaking, the story must be told in a fairly linear fashion, focusing on a small group of characters.

The screenwriter must do two primary things: find the story (because film is much more story-driven than the contemporary novel), and create a world for the audience to lose itself in.

Anthony Minghella, the talented writer-director of the Academy Award-winning film *The English Patient*, had this to say of the difficult process of adapting that complex literary novel to film: "The book is largely connected with the poetry and beauty of words, and film doesn't mainly work in verbal terms but with images. The job of the screenwriter is much more architectural than it is the work of poetry . . . What I tried to do was to find a way of translating [the author's] book not in a literal sense but in a way so that when I'd made the film it would have some of the lyricism that the book had."

The key is to find the book's essential theme, its core. With the story and the emotional core in place, the screenwriter has to make choices: which elements, incidents and characters to keep or to combine from the book, and which to jettison in favor of telling the story as effectively as possible. Imagine taking a book that's several hundred pages long, with dozens of characters, and trying to fit it into a two-hour movie where the audience expects to see the star onscreen most of the time. There simply isn't time in a movie to include all a novel's characters and subplots.

Paul Attanasio, the screenwriter of *Quiz Show* and *Donnie Brasco* (both true-life stories), says, "I try to really figure out who these people are, and which events [from the book] make scenes that reveal who these people are."

The focus must be on the protagonist and the major change he goes through.

Recently, I adapted two very different books, with very different challenges in terms of turning them into movies. The first, *Recessional*, is a best-selling novel by James Michener. Like all his novels, it's a big, entertaining story with a huge cast of characters and countless subplots. There were three overall challenges in adapting this book as a TV movie. First, how to condense it to a manageable length, which meant losing at least 75 percent of the story and most of the characters, primarily elderly people living in a retirement facility. Second, how to make the protagonist, the young doctor who's medical director of the facility, the kind of character that a bankable TV star would want to play. (The protagonist in the book simply wasn't interesting enough and didn't have a strong enough "arc," the growth and change a character undergoes.) And third, how to create a touching romance out of the rather grim romantic subplot in the book.

I addressed the first issue by selecting a few of the most interesting of the elderly characters to focus on, and eliminating the rest. Also, I addressed

95

only a couple of the many medical issues Michener touched upon.

The second problem was resolved by making the protagonist more complex and giving him a major character flaw to overcome by the end of the movie. This made him a much more fascinating character for an actor to play.

The third problem was actually the most difficult. The young woman in the book who was the romantic interest of the doctor was totally unsuitable for film. (She was horribly mutilated in the book and there was no way a network was going to allow that in a movie.) I had to create an entirely new character for this heroine. However, I was inspired by another female character in the book. I saw that many of that character's qualities would work perfectly for the heroine, because they put her at odds with the hero. Conflict is the essence of drama.

As you can see, I made significant changes in the story, not only to make it work as a movie but to *sell* it as a movie. This is very common. Once an author has signed a contract to sell the film rights to his book, he has no control at all in what is done to that story. Author Tom Clancy, who has seen several of his best-selling thrillers become movies that he didn't necessarily like, bitterly likened this process to "selling your daughter into prostitution."

The second book I adapted was much less challenging and required fewer changes because it was a shorter, simpler story that worked remarkably well for film. *'Twas the Night Before* by Jerry B. Jenkins is a romantic Christmas fantasy about a young woman of tremendous faith who believes in Santa Claus, and the young man she falls in love with, who is cynical and believes in almost nothing. By the end of the book, he has found a profound faith, and even believes in Santa. The heartwarming, beautifully told story was perfect for a network Christmas movie.

The problem was that there was no child in it. By definition, a network Christmas movie is family-oriented. There must be a child, or children, in it. Because of the way the book was written, it was remarkably easy to insert a child in the story. The heroine in the book is a university professor. I simply made her a grammar school teacher and made one of her young students a significant character.

With both books, the adaptations were designed to fashion stories of the right length with castable main characters who would appeal to bankable stars.

The Roadmap

Here, step by step, is a roadmap for adapting a book.

- Begin with a logline of the story. Remember, a logline is a one- or two-sentence description of the story, focusing on the main characters, the setting and what's at stake.
- Write a brief outline, in just a few sentences, of each chapter. Go over this outline and discard anything that isn't essential to telling the story in the movie.
- Lift the most dramatic elements from these chapters and make sure they're placed in a confined time frame. Everything is abbreviated and consolidated.
- Organize the material in the most dramatic way—in ascending order of drama. (Each event is more dramatic than the preceding event, ending with the most dramatic event of all.)
- Divide these events into three sections that correspond to the traditional three-act structure of the movie. There should be a major turning point (an event that sends the story in a new direction and raises the stakes) at the end of Act One and Act Two. Act Three should have the climax and resolution.
- Focus on key characters. Eliminate extraneous characters. Combine similar characters.
- Introduce the protagonist immediately, and make sure he's onscreen most of the time.
- Use montages (a sequence of scenes tied together by a unifying theme or action) to condense events from the book. You can also use montages to show a passage of time, to tighten the time frame of the story.
- Make sure the setup is fast. Within the first ten pages of your screenplay, establish the main characters and the premise.
- Express any nonverbal thoughts of characters through action.
- Use very little narrative description in setting up the scenes.
- Generally speaking, make most scenes between one and one-half to three pages in length.
- Make sure most dialogue is no longer than five lines. Rarely use longer speeches.

If you can do all that, you will successfully adapt a book to screen.

PART THREE

Selling Your Screenplay

14 Pitching

What is a "pitch?" How do you go about it? And how does formulating a pitch help in writing your screenplay?

The American Heritage Dictionary of the English Language lists two definitions for the term "pitch." Both accurately describe the nervous reaction most writers have when faced with verbally presenting their story to a network, studio or production company: "To attempt to promote or sell, often in a high-pressure manner. To stumble around; lurch."

Most writers hate pitching their stories, but do it because it's a necessary evil. A few actually enjoy it and are terrific at it. Though I've never been an actress, I think it must be just like auditioning for a role. The only difference is that with a writer the potential buyer is rejecting your story, not you.

When you reach a certain level of experience and success as a screenwriter, you will often pitch a story before actually writing the screenplay. This saves time and effort if it's a story no one is going to respond to. If you're lucky, someone will respond to it and make a deal to pay you to write the script.

Beginning writers rarely have an opportunity to pitch their stories to buyers, so they might think it isn't necessary to know how to pitch. But there is strong value in learning about pitching, even if you won't be doing it for a buyer. Getting your story into "pitchable" form can help you work it out in the best possible way.

One highly successful writer describes his pitch process this way: First, he pitches the "one-liner," or logline (premise), so the buyer can immediately grasp the overall take. Then he pitches the general structure and story line (emphasizing act breaks and major plot points). Finally, he discusses the characters in detail.

Do you see how doing this before you write the script can help enormously? If you have a well-thought-out logline, structure, story line (with turning points) and thorough characterization, you'll be in good shape to write the script.

The essence of a pitch is brevity. The best pitches are only five to ten minutes long, which obviously means you can't convey most of the details of your story. If you think this is impossible to do, try this exercise: Pitch a movie you really like to a friend. You'll find that you do it quickly, passing over details and focusing on the main plot and the most important characters. You'll usually only spend a few minutes doing this, yet you'll get across the essence of the movie and why it was appealing.

You should be able to do this same thing with your own story.

Winning Pitches

When you do find yourself in the nerve-wracking position of pitching your story to a producer or executive, here are tips to make the experience as successful and enjoyable as possible.

- Get a good night's sleep the night before. You want to be rested and refreshed.
- Research the subject matter of your story so that you can not only write about it knowledgably, but discuss it intelligently, as well.
- Know your buyer. Don't pitch a suspense-thriller to an executive who's only looking for high-concept comedies.
- Be prepared—rehearse your pitch.
- First, begin with the title, genre and theme. Orient the listener to the time and place of your story.
- Have a strong premise.
- Be very visual in the opening. Give a sense of how the movie will look at the beginning. ("We open on a beautiful mountain valley. A magnificent herd of wild mustangs come thundering toward the camera.")
- Intersperse your telling of the story with brief snippets of dialogue.
- Have a "beat sheet" (a list of the most important plot points) with you, to jog your memory, in case you get nervous and lose your place as you're telling the story.
- Have your story pitch worked out in three acts.
- Go into the setup of your story in greater detail than you do with the remainder of the movie. Describe the characters quickly but completely. Then sketch acts two and three with less detail, focusing on the most dramatic or critical events.

- Be passionate about your story. Buyers respond to the passion a writer feels for a story. Tell why you are utterly certain this will be a wonderful movie that audiences will respond to.
- Have an answer to the question, "Why should we buy this movie? What audience is it for?"
- If possible, take an acting class to learn how to physically present yourself and tell a story with real energy and drama.
- Watch the reaction of the person you're pitching to. Look at his body language. It will reveal if he's interested or if you're losing his interest.
- Don't argue with the buyer. Even if you disagree with a comment or suggestion he makes, simply thank him for his interest and say, "That's very interesting. Let me think about that."
- Tailor the pitch to the person you're pitching to. If you're pitching to an actor, he'll be most interested in the character he would play in your movie. So you focus the pitch on the development of this character and his arc. If you're pitching to a network or studio executive, or producer, focus on the story and why it's a "market-driven idea."
- Dress in a comfortable but stylish manner. "Casual chic" is the essence of Hollywood. (A designer blazer over faded jeans is practically a uniform, whether you're a man or a woman.)
- Do not take longer than ten or fifteen minutes at the very most to tell your story.
- Don't get into the nuts-and-bolts details of your story. Save those for the questions that the executive will, hopefully, ask after your pitch is over.
- Be prepared to leave behind a treatment for the buyer to look over later.
- Don't expect the buyer to give a yes or no in the meeting. On rare occasions that does happen, but normally the person you're pitching to will have to submit the project to his boss for approval.

Sample Pitch

Following is a story that my collaborator, Madeline DiMaggio, and I pitched. This is a particularly succinct pitch, but it gets across the story.

A Deadly Defense

Erotic suspense/thriller.

Judith Sutton, an unhappy, psychologically abused wife, discovers her

101

husband murdered. She is the prime suspect. A longtime family friend and successful defense attorney, Dan Halloran, agrees to take on the case. He is the only thing that stands between Judith's hope of freedom and a prison sentence, or possibly execution. He's attractive, caring and possesses a passionate belief in her innocence, despite the evidence against her. She finds herself falling in love with him.

Judith is released on bail. Her relationship with Dan, which begins as gentle and innocent, turns highly erotic and passionate. So much so that Judith starts to realize he's obsessed with her. She begins to suspect that he's the real killer. She investigates, learns she was right. Dan knew Judith would never leave her husband, and the only way he could have her was to kill her husband. He never meant to incriminate her—that was an accident.

Now Judith must convince the police and the D.A. that she's innocent and her attorney is guilty. But who will believe her? Suddenly, new evidence turns up that absolutely incriminates her. She knows that Dan, who she has rejected, is behind this. How can she prove her innocence when she knows he's about to throw the case in order to protect himself and convict her?

In the tense climax in the courtroom, Judith cleverly turns the tables on Dan and clears herself, at the same time proving his guilt.

Do you see how even in such a brief pitch, we know all the salient information about the story? The main characters, plot line, genre, twists and turns, and resolution are all here. In pitching it, we were prepared to go into all the details that we left out, if the buyer was interested. What you hope for when pitching is that the buyer will be drawn into the story enough that he will ask lots of questions when you've finished.

# 15 Coverage

Coverage is a written critique, following a standard format, that is done to almost every screenplay, book, play, treatment, etc. that is submitted to a network, studio or production company. Either a reader, whose sole job is doing coverage, or an assistant to an executive, will do this report. The executive will almost always read the coverage before reading the script. And if the coverage is critical, he won't bother with the script.

For obvious reasons, writers hate coverage. It is often an inaccurate critique of your script, by young and inexperienced readers. But there isn't anything that can be done about it. I'm discussing it now because it's important that you understand how the business works. The only good thing that can be said from learning about coverage is that it shows you how people in the business approach the scripts that are submitted to them—how they judge them and what they're looking for.

Here's coverage that was done on my unproduced screenplay, *Perfect Blonde*. (By the way, N/A means "not applicable." That generally means there are no "elements"—stars, director, producer, etc., attached.)

STORY DEPARTMENT COVERAGE

TITLE: PERFECT BLONDE

AUTHOR: PAM WALLACE (CLIENT)

GENRE: DRAMA/THRILLER

TYPE/DRAFT/PAGES: Screenplay/First Draft/106 pages

TIME/LOCALE: PRESENT/CHICAGO

VIA: N/A

STUDIO/NETWORK: N/A

SUBMITTED FOR: GENERAL CONSIDERATION

DIRECTOR: N/A

PRODUCER: N/A

TALENT: N/A

PROJECT STATUS: N/A

SUBMITTED TO: CNB

DATE: 1-25-99

CONCEPT: Several financial derivatives experts play high-stakes poker with their careers, trying to hit the jackpot by scheming to swindle a hundred million dollars from their firm and stabbing each other in the back.

SYNOPSIS

While charismatic derivatives specialist MATT THOMAS impresses his boss, CARL FRANKLIN, with his sales ability, bright and hardworking CARRIE SEGER struggles to get noticed. Both are surprised when they are called in to Franklin's office with goofy co-worker PETER MACALLISTER. Franklin puts Matt in charge of a hot new project to mine the most money possible out of Russian heavy crude oil, and Carrie is furious that she was passed over in the boy's-club scheme. Matt consoles Carrie and gets his team excited about the possibilities this project presents for their careers, working hard to overcome the limitations of his working-class upbringing. Carrie is upset when another FEMALE TRADER commits suicide, unable to handle the pressures of working for the firm. Franklin sends Matt on a vacation, and Matt is smitten by the beautiful JORDAN WEBB the moment he sees her. They slowly fall for each other and return to Chicago together as Jordan is impressed by Matt's power and money. When he returns, Matt jumps right into an all-night session with Carrie and Peter, readying the firm's position for the new project. But his focus is stolen away by the beautiful Jordan, using her sex appeal to wrap him around her finger. Peter is impressed with Jordan, but Carrie doesn't like her, convinced that she's bad news. Carrie resents Matt and Peter getting all the credit from the sexist Franklin, even though Matt and Peter sing her praises. Matt brings Jordan to a party at Franklin's penthouse suite, and she clashes with Carrie. Jordan makes Matt jealous by flirting with Franklin, pushing Matt to make more and more money to satisfy her hunger for material things. Carrie doesn't like the effect that Jordan has on Matt, who becomes consumed by making a killing on the new project.

The conservative Carrie worries that Matt is risking too much to please Jordan and suggests that he be more cautious. But big bonuses come from Franklin as Matt keeps pressuring clients to invest heavily in Russian heavy crude. Soon after, sparks fly between Jordan and Carrie when Jordan confronts Carrie about her lot at the firm. Franklin and Jordan both keep up the pressure on Matt to hit a home run, but Carrie is worried when Matt presents a bold plan to drive up the price of Russian crude to make the firm a mint. He works tirelessly to make his plan come to fruition, but he falls just short and costs the firm a hundred million dollars. Franklin fires Matt, who seems distraught. But when he meets Jordan, Matt is jubilant, having pulled a fast one on the firm to the tune of $100 million he put in a secret bank account for himself and Jordan. But later that night Jordan meets with Franklin, having planned the entire manipulation from the outset. Franklin murders Matt to cover his tracks, shocking Jordan. But when he's also fired, Franklin can't get his hands on the money. While Carrie is shocked to learn of Matt's "suicide," Jordan seduces Carrie, trying to win her help in getting to the money. Jordan admits that she's in collusion with Franklin, who instructs Carrie how to transfer the money to a safe account that they can access. But Carrie is suspicious when she finds that Jordan is a financial genius in her own right, merely playing dumb for convenience sake. Carrie shocks Peter when she admits that she is a lesbian. Meanwhile, Jordan tells Carrie that she is falling for her, and Carrie doesn't know what to believe. Carrie makes the transfer, but sends it to a different account, trying to double-cross Franklin. Jordan catches up with her, and they plan to run off together. The SEC are on to Franklin, but he eludes them, catches Jordan and Carrie, and threatens to kill them unless they transfer the money to his account. However, Carrie and Jordan turn the tables on Franklin, kill him and make off with their fortune, fleeing the country to live the rest of their lives together in the lap of luxury.

EVALUATION

Comments: Smartly conceived and nicely executed, this twisting and turning dramatic thriller has some engaging elements that make it a compelling read. Telling the story of the double-crosses between a group of financial derivative experts who try to make their fortune in the high-pressure/high-stakes market that they make their living in, the script is an intense and sexy endeavor that does a nice job of keeping you engaged over the long haul.

Wallace does a nice job of infusing this setting with intensity and high dramatic stakes, displaying a keen understanding of the world of financial derivatives. It's a world akin to high-stakes, legalized gambling, so the players in it are forced to take heavy risks to rise to the top. Those with the most guts see the most rewards, but also fall the furthest, as the script does a standout job of exploring the parameters for what it means to be successful in modern society.

But while the meat of the script is pretty strong, the one area where Wallace may need to do a little work is in more clearly defining exactly whose story this is supposed to be. The first three quarters of the story follow Matt as he takes the big risks, falls under the influence of the dangerous femme fatale (Jordan) and pays the ultimate price. But once Matt dies, the script continues to play out more narrative intrigue as the focus falls on Carrie, who has been a background player for the majority of the story to that point. If Carrie is the one who wins out in the end, we need to spend more time with her in the first seventy pages. Likewise, if we're supposed to be happy about her ending up with the manipulative and dangerous Jordan, then we need to see more of a distinct and believable change in her once she claims that she has fallen in love with Carrie. It seems like they don't have enough emotional interchange at this point for that to be believable.

Regardless, there's strong potential here as Wallace does a nice job of mixing the dangers of the financial world, the desperation of her characters and these characters' scheming for the big payoff into an intense ride. It is somewhat reminiscent of *Bound* in the way its characters are set up and in terms of its utilizing sex to give women the power they crave in the end. With that edgy sensibility, it has strong audience appeal, especially in arthouse circles, where its oblique tendencies can be fully appreciated.

Overall, there's some really nice things at work here. With a strong concept and engaging characters, it just needs a little focusing and refinement to make the most of the assets it possesses. A definite consider.

	EXCELLENT	GOOD	FAIR	POOR
CHARACTERS		X		
DIALOGUE		X		
STRUCTURE		X		
STORY		X		

RECOMMEND _____   CONSIDER ___X___   PASS _____

KEY LEAD BREAKDOWN

CARRIE SEGER: Female/30s. An attractive, but not beautiful, derivatives expert who specializes in number crunching. She is naturally conservative and secretly a lesbian, longing to break through the glass ceiling at her firm that keeps her down and in the closet.

MATTHEW THOMAS: Male/30s. A handsome and charismatic derivatives expert who has the gift of brilliant salesmanship. He is driven to reach awesome riches by his blue-collar upbringing, longing for a trophy wife and all the material trimmings.

108 **JORDAN WEBB:** Female/30s. A drop-dead gorgeous blonde with a knockout body and an insatiable appetite for the finer things in life. She works with Franklin

to manipulate Matt, making him think she loves him and convincing him to risk it all to make his killing. Actually a brilliant financial mind in her own right, she plays dumb because it is easier that way.

CARL FRANKLIN: Male/40s. A sadistic and manipulative vice president at Matt and Carrie's firm. He's their immediate boss and oppresses Carrie with his sexist attitudes. Willing to do whatever it takes to make his mint.

PETER MACALLISTER: Male/30s. An awkward and socially inept derivatives specialist who works on Carrie's and Matt's team. He has little luck with the ladies and longs to impress Jordan. Looks up to Carrie and Matt.

16 Agents and Marketing

Whew! You did it! You finished a screenplay. You worked hard on it, rewriting and polishing until it was as good as you could possibly make it. If possible, you've even gotten a professional critique. (I highly recommend my friend and occasional collaborator, Madeline DiMaggio, at P.O. Box 1172, Pebble Beach, CA 93953.) Now you're ready to try to sell it.

That's the hard part.

As difficult as it is to write a good script, it's even harder to sell it. But despite the obstacles, I truly believe that if a script is good enough (or at least commercial enough for the demands of the current market), and the writer is persistent enough in marketing it, the script will sell. That is no guarantee that it will get produced. The vast majority of screenplays that sell never get produced. That is one of the harshest realities of the film business. Nora Ephron, a tremendously talented and successful writer/director (*You've Got Mail*) said once that only about one out of every four screenplays she writes actually gets produced. She felt that was a good batting average—after all, she was batting .250.

The most important thing I want you to understand is that even if your screenplay doesn't sell, that doesn't mean it isn't good. In fact, the better the script, the harder it seems to be to sell. When you look at the scripts that win Academy Awards, most of them took years to sell. For instance, *Platoon* took more than ten years to sell. My screenplay for *Witness* took over three years to sell. It received more than its fair share of criticism along the way.

How does a screenplay get to the person who's in a position to buy it? Almost always through an agent or entertainment attorney. Unless you have a personal connection to someone in the film business, the only way to get your script read is by having an agent or attorney submit it. Most actors, studios, networks and production companies will return, unopened and unread, any script that is submitted to them "over the transom."

Stories about a waitress handing a script to an actor who was dining in the restaurant where she worked, and shortly thereafter making a six-figure sale, are rare to the point of being almost nonexistent. The reality is that you must market your screenplay in a professional manner. Approaching someone personally is unprofessional. They will rarely respond to that.

Screenplays get to actors by first going through their agents. Part of the agent's job is screening material submitted to the actor.

There is a significant exception to this rule: screenwriting fellowships and competitions. They are a great way to get around that high wall that surrounds Hollywood. When you apply for a fellowship or submit a script to a competition, your work is viewed by professionals in the industry. Often this leads to a sale, or at least getting an agent.

Getting an Agent

Other than competitions, how do you go about getting an agent? Unfortunately, it tends to be a vicious circle. You can't get an agent without having made your first sale, and you can't make your first sale without an agent. However, there is hope. Every year agents take on new writers, usually through personal recommendations, occasionally through reading a spec script that's submitted to them.

Based on my experience with agents, here are the answers to some of the questions most commonly asked of agents.

QUESTION: Is it better for a new writer to write a feature film spec script or an episode of a TV series?

ANSWER: It's better to write a movie script. Don't differentiate between feature film or TV movie. And don't put act breaks in it, even if you think it would be best as a TV movie. If a buyer is interested in it as a TV movie, it will be easy to insert act breaks.

QUESTION: Should you ever pay an agent to read your script?
ANSWER: No.

QUESTION: Is one script enough to show to an agent who's interested?
ANSWER: No. You should always have more than one, to prove that you're productive and not a "one-shot wonder."

QUESTION: When an agent agrees to look at your script, should you send a treatment along with it?

ANSWER: There is disagreement about this. Some agents feel you should, and some feel you shouldn't. Personally, I feel it's best not to send a treatment, unless it's been specifically requested. It's too easy for an agent to read the treatment and dismiss the story.

QUESTION: What do most agents look for in a script?

ANSWER: The same thing buyers look for: great dialogue, interesting characters, sound structure and a marketable premise.

QUESTION: What are big turnoffs for agents?

ANSWER: The same things that turn off buyers—an unprofessional-looking script, one that's very dense and doesn't have a lot of "white space," lots of camera directions.

QUESTION: How are agents paid?

ANSWER: They receive a percentage (usually 10 percent, sometimes 15) of the sale price of your screenplay.

QUESTION: What is a franchised agent?

ANSWER: One who subscribes to the Writers Guild of America's Basic Agreement between Artists and Managers. These agents deal with studios and producers who are signatories to the guild. (All writers must belong to the guild, once they've sold their first script.) Only look for a franchised agent.

QUESTION: How can you find a list of franchised agents?

ANSWER: The Writers Guild will provide it. Attending screenwriting conferences is also a good way to meet agents.

QUESTION: Do agents critique your work?

ANSWER: Rarely. There are professionals who will do this for a fee, but shop around to find a reputable one who won't charge an exorbitant fee. The Writers Guild magazine, *Written By*, usually carries ads for people who do script analysis and critique.

QUESTION: Should you include a cover letter when you submit a script to an agent?

ANSWER: Yes, but keep it brief. Don't talk about how brilliant the script is and how much the agent will love it. He'll want to make up his own mind about that. Only include information about yourself that is relevant to the script. For instance, if you've written a medical thriller and you're a physician, mention that.

QUESTION: Can any attorney serve as an entertainment attorney?

ANSWER: Technically, yes. But in actuality it's best to hire an experienced entertainment attorney. This kind of attorney basically only negotiates a contract for a writer. He doesn't usually market a script or become involved in a writer's career in any other way. There are two kinds of writers who use attorneys alone, without agents: First, a writer who's so successful that he is offered all the writing-for-hire work he could possibly want and doesn't need an agent to look for work for him. Second, a new writer who hasn't been able to get an agent but has gotten the interest of a reputable entertainment attorney.

What They're Looking For

Everyone in the film business—whether it's an agent considering a new client, an actor, or a buyer at a studio, network or production company—is looking for the same thing: A screenplay that is either so "high concept" that it will make a tremendously commercial movie even if it isn't especially well executed, or a screenplay that is so brilliantly written, so deeply touching and marvelously entertaining, that they fall in love with it, whether it's particularly commercial or not.

There are writers who manage to write and sell scripts they don't love. They're calculated efforts at marketing. But very few writers succeed this way. It's important to be aware of the market overall, what kind of movies are being made and why. But instead of focusing on what "they're" looking for and trying to write accordingly, the best marketing advice I can give to an aspiring writer is to write a screenplay you love, work hard on it and do the best job you possibly can, then be persistent in getting it to agents. With a little bit of luck, an agent will recognize that your script is just what someone is looking for. And the rest will be history. . . .

In this book, I've given you practical advice about the craft and the business of screenwriting. I'd like to conclude by offering a little personal advice.

Carefully observe the life around you. That means looking closely at your own life and the lives of others. The best writers are interested in, and knowledgeable about, psychology. After all, the basic goal of almost all writing is to help us understand the human condition better. This will give you something of value to say, a certain insight and perspective about life that you can communicate in your writing.

Don't try to mimic someone else's voice. Find your own. When Shane Black wrote the highly successful *Lethal Weapon*, aspiring writers everywhere were trying desperately to copy his particular style. It didn't work. Only Shane Black could write like Shane Black. Only you can write like you. Be the best "you" that you can be.

Recently, a screenplay titled *Steinbeck's Point of View* sold for more money than any other script in history. The studio that bought it didn't do so because it's "big" in any way. It's not a big budget, big special effects, big action extravaganza. It's actually a small, rather spiritual story. Ironically, the studio executive said he bought it because of the writer's "unique and powerful voice."

Nurture your own voice. Believe in yourself. And know that success as a screenwriter usually depends more on persistence, learning the craft and articulating your own special point of view than on talent.

Good luck!